The University: An Organizational Analysis

BLACKIE BOOKS ON ORGANIZATIONAL ANALYSIS

The Concept of Organization
The Hospital: An Organizational Analysis
The School: An Organizational Analysis
The University: An Organizational Analysis

The University:
An Organizational Analysis

Hugh Livingstone

BLACKIE: Glasgow and London

0 216 89744 0 (Paperback)
0 216 89705 X (Hardback)

Blackie and Son Limited
Bishopbriggs, Glasgow G64 2NZ
5 Fitzhardinge Street, London W1H 0DL

Printed by Thomson Litho, East Kilbride, Scotland

Contents

Acknowledgements

Most of my ideas on organizational analysis have been formed in collaboration (or conflict) with my close colleagues at Strathclyde for the past five years and more, Roy Wilkie, David Bradley, and Nicholas Perry. As a result, I hesitate to claim any of the ideas expressed in this book as wholly my own. More specifically, Roy Wilkie has encouraged me throughout the writing of the book and has commented extensively on the original draft. David Bradley read most of the original and I am grateful for his comments on chapter 2. Unfortunately, it was not possible for Nicholas Perry to read the manuscript, but I am aware that my account of the process of 'professionalization' and my typology of students, both in chapter 5, owe a lot to seminars we have held in the past. Jill Wilkie also read most of the original manuscript and her suggestions greatly improved the style.

My thoughts on the implications of 'course teams' at the Open University were first suggested at a seminar at Strathclyde at which Professor Gerald Fowler described how they worked. Similarly, my interest in the proposals of the Birmingham University Review Body stems from the many interesting discussions I have had with Sir Maurice Dean.

The final responsibility for all that appears is, of course, mine alone. My thanks are also due to Mrs. A. Alexander for typing some of the drafts, and especially to Mrs. Patricia McTaggart who typed the rest of the drafts and completed the final manuscript with great speed and accuracy.

Lastly, my thanks to Joan, my wife, who not only helped to find time for me to work on the book, but has also had to tolerate my somewhat variable demeanour throughout the summer.

CHAPTER 1

The University as an Organization

What is the university? A set of buildings? An idea? A society? A concept? All of these are terms that have been used in discussing universities. Our perspective is that the greatest understanding of what a university is, can be gleaned from viewing it as an organization. By approaching it as a social grouping of human beings whose activities are consciously co-ordinated and controlled in order to achieve some specific purpose, we will be better able to understand the problems that affect the contemporary British university. But what kind of organization is the university? It has been described as a community, as a monastery, as a bureaucracy, as a political system, a business corporation, even as a kind of factory, as just an extension of school. Our first task is to look at the more important frames of reference that are currently employed, or have been in the past employed by writers and commentators who have tried to capture the essence of a university's organizational characteristics. These may be summarized as 'models' of universities, a simplification of reality which emphasizes essential features.

The traditional assumption about the organization of a university is that it is fundamentally a *community* of scholars. The very word university, in medieval latin *universitas*, meant simply community. Indeed, to make sense the word had to be qualified in order that its meaning would be clear, viz. *universitas disciplorum et magistrorum* (community of masters and pupils), or *universitas scholarium* (community of scholars). Historically, this model derives mainly from the supposed values of an Oxford or Cambridge college. Today the staunchest supporters of this model usually have strong connections with Oxbridge, and the nearest this model comes to reality is an Oxbridge-style college.

A university run on community assumptions sees no basic conflict between arts and sciences, between teacher and taught. Indeed, there is usually built into this model the assumption that pastoral care of students is important and that the social experience of university should extend beyond mere acquisition of knowledge.

Because of its historical association with Oxbridge, this model usually assumes a strong teaching-orientation. Its ideals are usually assumed to have attained most eloquent exposition by Cardinal Newman in 1852. To him the university was "the high protecting power of all knowledge and science". If the object of a university were "scientific and philosophic discovery, I do not see why a university should have any students", he wrote,[1] a sentiment apparently shared by substantial numbers of twentieth century staff, to judge by the comments of their students! The teaching orientation is still an important undercurrent, especially in Arts faculties, although its adherents rarely attack the currently dominant view that research is the real business of a university. For example, one of the 'great men' of recent times, the philosopher A. D. Lindsay, who in 1948 forsook the cloisters of Balliol College, Oxford where he had been Master for some twenty-five years, to head the new University College of North Staffordshire, felt impelled to ask one of his science professors complaining of lack of time for research, "What do you want to do research for?", thereby rendering his colleague speechless.[2]

Many of the assumptions of the community model are, however, incorporated in the viewpoint of those normally critical of many Oxbridge values in general and of the real or imagined teaching ethos in particular. For example, the American, Abraham Flexner, who between the wars articulated the notion of the research-oriented university, thought of the university as an organism, its parts inextricably bound together.[3] Indeed, the community model derives a lot of its potency from having been embraced by the research-oriented. The apparent impossibility of harmony between the research-minded teachers and would-be students does, of course, lead to this model being perhaps too readily dismissed as impracticable.

To many students in particular, the assumptions of the community model seem absent from the universities they attend. They charge that universities are essentially *bureaucratic* organizations. Now, to most people, bureaucracy is a dirty word.

It is associated with organizations that are big, impersonal and unpleasant. To the social scientist however, the word bureaucracy describes only the simple truth that as organizations grow and become more complex, more formal systems of regulation replace the informal understanding that is often sufficient for effective co-ordination in the smaller, simpler units. In particular, rules have to be formulated and applied. They have to apply to all without exception and are, therefore, impersonal. The activities carried out by any one person become more and more specialized and co-ordination is best achieved by means of a hierarchy or 'pyramid' of authority, with each person or unit in turn accountable to only one other person or unit. These are characteristics of many organizations. We ourselves have observed how family firms go through a process of 'bureaucratization' as they grow larger. It is a process normally associated, contrary to popular mythology, with efficiency. Indeed, one of the reasons why bureaucracies are disliked is because of the efficiency with which unpaid bills or income tax returns are not forgotten. If no action is taken, the machine will grind remorselessly on. It is the sense of powerlessness that makes bureaucracies unpopular, not the eagerly-seized examples of 'inefficiency' which can result from over-rigid rules.

Obviously, as universities have grown larger, an element of bureaucratization has occurred. To the student, the matriculation process often appears to be geared to reducing his identity to a computerized number on a plastic card. Some of the older American universities simply refuse to computerize their student records on principle, as they sense the symbolic depersonalization that this process represents. In the larger universities, it sometimes appears to the student that he is 'learning-unit 2075062973', which enrols for, attends at, and takes his examinations in, subject 64 207. And this sense of remoteness may be shared by staff, especially junior staff. The university is, therefore, perceived as an administrative hierarchy controlling a system where numbered students are enrolled for numbered classes, taught by nameless teachers and examined by faceless professors.

In Britain, it is perhaps hard to accept that the above represents reality. The degree of bureaucratization in universities is usually far below that of other organizations of similar size. Nevertheless, to students whose reference point is the more personalized school, the sense of isolation in the university can be devastating. Most universities do try to counter the impersonality of the large organization by using tutorial teaching methods and various forms of student counselling. We have to recognize, however, that a bureaucratic model has recently been appropriate for much of Western Europe and, to a lesser extent, of North America, and occasionally has some validity in Britain.

The perspectives that see the university primarily as a teaching or research community contain a strong element of isolationism. There are those, however, who see the university as having an active role in the community. This view of the university, which has been labelled the *service station* model by its detractors, sees the university going out to serve its public, seeking out its clients and giving them what it thinks they want. Clearly this perspective is less concerned with internal patterns of organization than with its relationships with its environment.

This view found its best expression in the efforts of genuinely idealistic men at American state institutions. Clark Kerr has quoted[4] the example of the University of Wisconsin at the turn of the century, where with the support of the state's formidable U.S. Senator, Robert La Follette, the university openly supported reform programmes, lobbied the state legislature, supported the trade unions and moved out into the farms with its agricultural extension courses. It became what it said it was, Wisconsin's university.

This orientation has always been strongly held in American 'public' universities. Their aim was always to serve the surrounding community. Not only do most have 'open entry' to all who wish to study there, they are also willing to teach or conduct research in any area that may serve a local interest.

The influence of this tradition has been immense in North America. Even the academically prestigious 'private' universities took on something of this mission, much to the disgust of Flexner, who published the fact[5] that even Chicago and Columbia awarded Master's degrees for theses such as *Photo‾ graphic Studies on Boiled Icing,* and *Buying Women's Garments‾ by Mail.* Today we can see at least two main expressions of this concept. The first is the existence in American university syllabi of overtly vocational programmes in subjects which in Britain would be held to be of dubious educational value, e.g.

physical education, home economics, secretarial science, journal-
ism, etc. Secondly, there is the awareness among American
industry and commerce of the skills and facilities that can be
utilized in universities. American firms frequently site their
plants in order to be near a campus which contains skills and
facilities that can be useful to them.

In Britain, some universities, particularly the former Colleges
of Advanced Technology, attempt to make many of their
courses 'practical' and 'relevant', in a similar way. Even they,
however, have to hawk their wares around British industry in
order to attempt to persuade firms to use their facilities and
expertise. Despite the indifference of industry, however, the
service station notion appeals to governments and will
undoubtedly be with us for a long time to come.

A further viewpoint on the nature of the university comes
from the student radicals or revolutionaries who were prominent
for some time after 1968. Theirs is unmistakably a *conflict*
model. They view the present system as a factory, where
students are a form of raw material, being processed and
delivered, duly packaged, into the capitalist job-market. One
expression[6] of this self-styled 'radical' viewpoint claimed that
only four groups have a functional role in universities. These
were teachers, researchers, students and technical staff. Amongst
these groups there should be 'social equality' as an 'elementary
democratic right'. One might have expected adherents of such
an overtly egalitarian view to remember that administrators,
like policemen, are workers too. This model is seen by the
'militants' as inherently and spontaneously conflictual. There
exists an inevitable conflict of interests over matters such as
allocation of teaching, forms of instruction, hours of work, use
of university funds and facilities. In this conflict-situation
students should not be 'conned' into schemes giving them a
'share' in university government. Participation is a discreet form
of suffocation, they perceptively notice. What matters is not
the institutional charter, but the balance of forces. As one
'radical' put it, 'it is their capacity for mass struggle which
will make students a decisive force on or off campus, that staff
and administration will be obliged to reckon with'.[7] This view
exhibits the intellectual poverty of the extremist viewpoint.
There is no pretension to democracy. The decision-taking

medium is the mass-meeting, and the underlying ideology has undertones of the totalitarian concept of the 'general will' or the 'dictatorship of the proletariat'. Moreover, the balance of forces in this model is based on power. It is, however, hard to discover just what power students are supposed to possess, other than the support of public or parliamentary opinion.

A more realistic view of the university sees relationships as much more complex than any of those outlined above. This *pluralistic* view was possibly best expressed in Clark Kerr's famous analysis and popularization of the 'multi-versity'.[8] The scale of the model Kerr had in mind has yet to reach Great Britain. Even in 1963 when he made his analysis, the University of California, of which he was then President (Vice-Chancellor), had 60,000 students in over 100 locations. It had an annual operating expenditure of $500 million and capital projects of $100 million. It had 40,000 employees, more than I.B.M., and was the world's largest purveyor of white mice. In 1972, the University of California had 111,000 students, but was far from being the largest American university. The largest was New York State with over 230,000 students, at which figure the British academic mind can only boggle.

Kerr's point, however, is that whereas the original medieval concept of the university was of a single community of masters and students with common interests, the modern university is composed of several or many separate communities with, in many cases, divergent interests. The university is divided both horizontally and vertically. There are vertical divisions separating the community of the pure scientists from that of the engineer, that of the arts man, that of the social scientist, and so on. Even within broad fields, civil engineers might have little to do with electrical engineers and sociologists might have little to do with psychologists. There are, more obviously perhaps, the horizontal divisions of status, undergraduates, graduate students, junior lecturers, professors, each a community of its own. In addition, we may identify communities of the non-academic personnel, administrators, secretaries, technicians and the like, and possibly the community of the graduates. Kerr made the point that Flexner had thought of the university as an organism with its parts inextricably linked. In the modern university, parts can be added or subtracted without anyone

noticing. He quoted one definition of a university as a series
of separate schools and departments held together by a central
heating system and added that a more up-to-date one might be
"a series of individual professors/entrepreneurs held together
by a common grievance over parking".[9]

The overall point is that in Newman's reference group, the
medieval village, each man has common interests; but in the
modern city of learning, interests frequently conflict. In this
plural society, the aims of the constituent groups may have
little to connect them. In such an organization, provision has
to be made for some agency to keep it in some kind of balance
or equilibrium. It is pointless in this situation to achieve a
false unity of purpose by defeating or promoting sectional
groups. The only way to ensure the long-run equilibrium, or
stability, of such an organization is by trying to control the
activities of constituent parts and to achieve some kind of
consistent, if ever-changing, balance. No university in Britain
faces the organizational problems of the American state universities. Yet in larger non-collegiate universities this pluralistic
model is an appropriate frame of reference. In the smaller
universities, mostly located in smaller towns, there is some
indication that the community or collegiate model, as it is sometimes called, has some relevance. Even there however, modest
growth can bring increased specialization and bureaucratization. Sussex University, for example, which was going to
're-draw the map of learning' by abolishing barriers between
subjects and which appointed teachers to schools rather than
departments, has, in the view of a number of its teachers,
reneged on its earlier commitments, and departments based
upon subject areas are reducing the scope of inter-disciplinary
activity. Even in the early years of a small institution like
Keele, where the idea of a common first year for both arts
and science undergraduates was, and is, a brave and isolated
attempt to cross disciplinary barriers, mutual incomprehension
of purpose among many arts and science staff was common.

A further development of the pluralistic model is a standpoint
which suggests that each of the different groups, which may
have opposing interests, actively engages in a political process
to strengthen its own position. This *political* model sees the
distribution of power in the university as the critical factor.

Analysis concentrates upon the nature, sources, and distribution of power in the organization.

In adopting a political perspective, one analyst[10] has suggested that first of all one has to identify the social structure of the organization, and the values, interests and goals of the different groups within the structure. Secondly, one has to recognize how pressures from these groups are articulated, and how they influence the decision process. Examples of this would be groups of senior academics leaking to the Press aspects of a university's plans or activities to which they are opposed, when they feel that opinion outside the university is more likely to share their view. It could take the form of student boycotts, demonstrations or 'sit-ins' to publicize a grievance and put pressure on those responsible for it to rectify it. The next stage is to analyse how the interests thus articulated become policies. This has been termed the legislative stage. A major task of legislative bodies is to respond to pressures and, out of the conflict situation, to create a feasible policy. This process is characterized by negotiation and 'horse-trading' until the policy is decided. The next stage, policy formulation, commits the organization to new goals. Lastly, there is the phase of policy execution. In this stage it is possible that those who lost something by the final decision may use the new pressures and interests created by the new policy to regain their position, thereby setting the whole process off again. There are obvious attractions in adopting this standpoint. Within universities there are many who adhere to a 'conspiracy' theory of organization and consider that universities are particularly fertile breeding grounds for cabals to combine to achieve their aims. Indeed, part of our argument in viewing existing university structures of government is that these can only be effective when 'politicking' precedes the decision process, where the 'real' meeting is always held before the formal one.

It appears to us that there is some degree of truth in all of the models we have outlined, when applied to most British universities. Although we would argue that one cannot often identify institutions where the *community* model accords with reality, nevertheless it has to be recognized that many staff and administrators do aspire towards it. In our view, the *pluralistic* model gives the most accurate description of the current reality, and suggests the general orientation with which we should approach university organization. We hesitate to adopt a *political* model, mainly because a great many activities are carried on in the university which have little to do with the political process. The political model undoubtedly illuminates one important aspect of government and administration in academic institutions, and the framework of analysis we have adopted in this book helps to illuminate the social structure, legislative process and goal-setting procedures of universities, which are all important aspects of the political model.

[handwritten margin note: But the political process may be analytically prior?]

Our intention is to analyse the general pattern of government and organization of British universities, in terms of how they hang together as organizations. Our earlier definition of an organization indicates that the key questions to be asked in understanding an organization are: What are its goals? How are they established? How are its activities structured? What are the values and orientations of its members? How is it controlled in order that goals are achieved? What technology does it employ?

By adopting this framework, we describe and explain the workings of the British university. We do not try to find any answers, although we cannot help drawing conclusions from our analysis. Organizational analysis is not a 'how-to-do-it' technique. The main intention of the approach is to indicate the set of factors which have to be considered before any judgement has a fair chance of validity. By adopting the framework of organizational analysis, we scorn those who pretend that administration can be an exact science. We try only to find a framework which ensures that judgement may be less haphazard.

In analysing the university as an organization, we try to understand what are its goals, objectives and purposes, and how these are viewed at different levels, how its various activities are co-ordinated, how relationships between individuals and groups are structured, and what are the characteristics and values of its members. These factors are interrelated. A change in one will affect the others. Moreover, additional effects will result from the nature of the methods used to achieve the goals (the 'technology'), and from the environment in which it operates. There has, therefore, to be some consistency between the objectives of the organization, the manner in which activities are co-ordinated and controlled, the values and orientations of the participants and the environment in which the organization operates. There are no universal principles of organizations. A tennis club and a prison cannot be organized on similar lines.

An obvious example is the effect of the environment. Our analysis is of the British university. Throughout we assume a particular social, economic, political and cultural framework when we discuss goals, structure, or values of members. Our discussion of the academic freedom of the individual pre-supposes a society whose political freedom is an assured right. One cannot discuss freedom to pursue research when many fields of possible enquiry are forbidden by *diktat*. One cannot discuss the nature of authority relations within the university when the state frequently intervenes in university affairs. Our analysis can have no relevance to universities in societies such as Spain, Greece, the Soviet Union or Cuba and many others, except to indicate a model against which they may be compared.

Within the British context, it seems appropriate to adopt an organizational view of universities, since in recent years many of them have felt compelled to hold inquiries into various aspects of their internal relationships, particularly those with their students. Some, including Birmingham, London and Oxford have held semi-independent inquiries into the nature of their purposes, government, organization and external relations. This questioning may be partly the result of a confusion of identity. Between the wars and even until the early sixties, the university scene in Britain was fairly static and events predictable. Between the establishment of the University College of Hull in 1927 and that of the University of Sussex in 1961, only one new institution was founded. Between 1961 and the inclusion of St. David's College, Lampeter, into the University of Wales in 1969, there was an outburst of new foundations, translations of existing institutions to university status, and the division of two-campus universities, amoeba-like, into separate institutions. In very broad terms, we may say that in 1962 there were twenty-one universities in Great Britain; by 1970 there were forty-four. These figures have to be considerably qualified, however, since only eight were completely new institutions. Moreover, the methods of computation adopted counts the universities of Wales and of London as one each, and thereby manages to 'lose' those colleges which were incorporated in them when upgraded to full university status.

The expansion in university education in the 1960s was without precedent. Between 1960/1 and 1970/1, university expenditure grew at twice the rate of Gross National Product. During that decade the number of students attending universities rose from 107,700 to 228,000. In a further ten years, current plans lead to a figure of 375,000 places in 1980/81. Even in 1970/71, however, thousands of would-be applicants who held the traditional minimum entry qualifications (2 advanced Level passes in the General Certificate of Education in England and Wales, 3 Higher Grade passes in the Scottish Certificate of Education in Scotland), failed to gain a place. The inability of universities to offer places to all those seeking them has stimulated an even faster rate of growth in local authority controlled further education. Even in the four years since 1966, when the then Secretary of State for Education, Mr. Anthony Crosland, first announced government support for the local authority sector, the number of students following degree courses in further education colleges rose from 23,720 to 42,723. In some other areas of higher education, for example in the colleges of education where numbers grew from 30,000 in 1960/61 to 93,500 in 1970/71, growth has been even faster than in the universities. This growth is the result of a remarkable social phenomenon, the tendency for a larger and larger proportion of each age group to stay on at school and to seek some form of higher education. Much of the planning for expansion in the sixties was done to meet the larger number of candidates from the 'bulge' of children born in the immediate post-war years which reached its peak around 1966/68. But as a result of the trend for more children to stay at school, demand for places did not slacken off after the 'bulge' passed. For example, the percentage of all seventeen year olds still at school in 1960 was 11.1, in 1965 it was 13.9, and by 1970 it was 20.2.

Traditionally, higher education meant university education. Today, in terms of numbers, universities account for just over half the students in higher education. Virtually all university students are, however, following degree-level courses, while this applies only to a minority of other students in higher education.

B

Moreover, despite verbal boosting of the local authority colleges by Ministers of the Crown, there are no perceptible challengers to university hegemony in higher education, in terms of intellectual status, social prestige and political influence.

In Great Britain as a whole, it is convenient to group the universities into categories which share the same broad characteristics. The categories are arbitrary, and some institutions do not fit well into any one category. First of all, the ancient English universities of Oxford and Cambridge are different from the others in size, organization, wealth, social origins of students, indeed in almost every respect. Secondly, the larger (and older) civic universities of England and Wales, having their origins in nineteenth century foundations. Chronologically the first of these was Durham which is, however, collegiate, not very big, and not in a large city. The large civic universities are usually thought to be Manchester, Birmingham, Liverpool, Leeds, Sheffield, Bristol. We should also include Newcastle, formerly a college of Durham University, and the University of Manchester Institute of Science and Technology (U.M.I.S.T.).

Thirdly, there are the smaller, and younger, civic universities, all of which started life as colleges offering London University degrees. These are Reading, Nottingham, Southampton, Hull, Exeter, Leicester. To these might be added the tiny St. David's College, Lampeter, now part of the University of Wales. The federal universities of Wales and London are perhaps a separate category, although all of the colleges of Wales fit the characteristics of the two civic categories. London, however, is a case apart, a combination of some forty-four colleges, specialized schools and institutions, and teaching hospitals. Its larger colleges fit into either of the civic categories, but the rest defy comparison. Fifthly, there are the new, post-war foundations. Keele started life in 1948 as a university college offering Manchester degrees, but all the others were fully independent right from their foundation. The others, which have been called the 'Shakespearian Seven' are Sussex, Essex, York, East Anglia, Kent, Lancaster and Warwick. Lastly, there are the former colleges of advanced technology (the 'ex-C.A.T.s') upgraded upon the recommendation of the Committee on Higher Education chaired by Lord Robbins, whose report in 1963 has been the reference point for virtually all discussion of higher education ever since.[11] These are now known as Aston, Bath, Bradford, Brunel, City, Loughborough, Surrey and Salford. In addition, the Chelsea college joined the University of London and the Cardiff one joined the University of Wales.

The Scottish universities are usually considered a separate category, largely in deference to the ancient four which have the peculiarity of drawing their powers from Acts of Parliament rather than from Royal Charter. The oldest, St. Andrews, is small, residential and collegiate in character. The other three ancient foundations, Glasgow, Aberdeen, and Edinburgh, resemble the large civics, as do Strathclyde, which historically has many similarities to U.M.I.S.T., and Dundee which devolved from St. Andrews in the same way as Newcastle from Durham. Stirling is a new foundation and Heriot-Watt, although it used to offer some Edinburgh University degrees, has similarities to the ex-C.A.T.s. For simplicity, the figures we have used in this book exclude the universities of Northern Ireland. Although there are several qualifications to be made in their case, they are very much part of the British university system. The Queen's University of Belfast is a large civic university, and the University of Ulster a new foundation.

Given the expansion of recent years as outlined above, it is clear that the word 'university' in Britain does not apply to a homogeneous type of institution. Even the above outline indicates the considerable variety which exists among British universities. Without careful qualification, generalizations are clearly dangerous. Bearing this in mind we now examine the key areas in the organization of universities.

CHAPTER 2

University Goals

"What are universities for, anyway?"[12] asked Lord Annan, Provost of University College, London, in the first Dimbleby lecture on BBC television in 1972. It is not entirely clear from the text of his polemical answer whether the 'anyway' signified puzzlement or aggression in the mind of his hypothetical questioner. Both qualities are certainly found in abundance in the popular mind when the subject of universities is discussed. And bewilderment can certainly be found even when the subject of a university's purpose is raised within the very walls of universities.

Every organization, every human institution, has a goal towards which it strives. Otherwise there would be no institution. Having a purpose is inherent in the notion of organization. Organizations are formed by human beings to fulfil purposes which cannot be achieved, or achieved very well, by one individual acting alone. Plans are made, duties allocated, responsibility for achieving sub-goals assigned, to individuals or to groups of individuals. Some method of achieving overall co-ordination is devised, in order that the activities undertaken lead to the achievement of the original purpose. Whether the organization is a tennis club, a residents' amenity association, a choir, a business firm, a trade union, a prison, the fundamental process of organization has this broad pattern. The means used to assign activities and ensure adequate performance vary greatly, depending upon the goal of each particular organization. Frequently the goal of an organization is not spelled out in formal terms. Those who join a golf club hardly need to ask what the club exists for. Those who take up employment in a business firm rarely enquire what purpose the firm has, since the everyday assumptions we make about business organizations are usually adequate for our understanding of the organization of tasks and persons within a firm. There was a time when the universities' function was also more or less assumed. Universities existed to train students for the older professions, law, teaching, the church, medicine.

These purposes were not uniform. The ancient English universities of Oxford and Cambridge were often seen as extensions of private education for gentlemen as well as training schools for Anglican clergy. In Scotland, the student body was always socially more heterogeneous and the purpose of higher education was always assuredly vocational, without the social trappings and expense of Oxbridge college life. The English provincial universities were founded to bring the benefits of the Scottish experience to those disqualified from entry to Oxford and Cambridge by religious tests, and to train students in the skills of science and engineering. Furthermore, there was little questioning of the social function of universities because the numbers of students attending them were few and much of the financing was private. Although most of the university-level institutions founded in England and Wales in the nineteenth century were dependent from the outset upon public funds from municipal and central government, the sums involved were small. It was not until 1919 that the government felt it necessary to institutionalize the provision of funds for universities by establishing the University Grants Committee. In 1919 the sum to be distributed to all the universities of Great Britain and Ireland, except Oxford and Cambridge, was £1 million. By 1945 this sum for Great Britain alone, now including Oxford and Cambridge, had grown to only £2.8 million. In 1955 the sum was £22 million. By 1965, however, it had grown to £170 million and in 1975 it will exceed £310 million. That the purpose of the distribution of such funds is the subject of public discussion and public scrutiny is hardly surprising.

What is the purpose of this expenditure? Lord Annan claimed that the answer was simple. "Universities exist to promote the life of the mind. They have two main roles. They should create and discover new knowledge and this they should do through reflection and research. They also exist to transmit to each generation a high culture. Whatever at a given time is thought to make men and women civilized, whatever is thought to be intellectually important and of concern to society they teach to their students."[13] Here Lord Annan is describing what universities ought to do, not what they are doing now. More importantly, there is no mention of *how* these aims are to be attained. Most statements about purposes of universities have similar short-comings. University charters contain bald statements that universities are about teaching and research and then go on to describe administrative structures and regulations without there being any apparent connection between them. Present-day discussions in Great Britain about the goals of universities usually begin with the statement on the aims of a system of higher education made by the Robbins Committee in 1963.

Their Report stated that any properly balanced system had four aims. These were, first, "instruction in skills suitable to take part in the general division of labour"; secondly, that "what is taught should be taught in such a way as to promote the general powers of the mind, the aim being to produce not mere specialists, but cultivated men and women"; thirdly, "the advancement of learning"; and finally, "the transmission of a common culture and common standards of citizenship".[14] There is in these formulations no suggestion of how these goals are to be achieved, or how one is to know if they are being achieved. In other words, they are brave statements of intent but of no operational value to those whose task it is to achieve these objectives.

We have already suggested that every organization has objectives as its very *raison d'être*. They have, one analyst has suggested, three major functions. First of all, goals provide a general guide to activity. A member of an organization who is aware of the organization's goal is better able to make his activities relevant to achieving it. Secondly, goals serve as a source of legitimacy. Activities can be justified if they can be shown to further achievement of the goals. Thirdly, they are a means of measuring success. This introduces the notion of effectiveness. An organization is effective if it achieves its objectives. It is important to distinguish this idea of effectiveness from that of efficiency, which is simply a measure of cost per unit of output. In terms of these three functions, the statements on university goals we have looked at can perhaps be held to satisfy the first one, that of general orientation, and possibly the second, that of legitimacy, but certainly not the third, that of a measure of organizational effectiveness. What we are suggesting is that if any assertion of a university goal is to be meaningful, there must be some means of judging its attainability. This does not demand precise measurement, but simply an indication of relative success.

✔ The formal goals of a university will be usually set out in its Charter. They could, however, be expanded by any body with the necessary authority to do so, such as the Court or Council, or, within the limits of their authority, by any academic body. It is proper to refer to the formal goals of a department, provided these relate to the wider goals of the institution. Frequently, however, it happens that formal goals become distorted at the trivial levels. Degree regulations, for instance, which may be formulated by teaching staff as providing useful guidelines for courses of study, frequently become inflexible chains which are impossible to break or even rattle without involving the highest authorities. Once 'proper procedures' become established, they tend to persist long after their usefulness has passed. At the more serious level, the recent need for stringent economy in the running of universities leads to increased power for those handling university finances and to decisions being taken simply on grounds of cost without regard to wider implications, i.e. efficiency becomes more important than effectiveness.

In any organization, however, the formal, official goals are not the only ones that are followed. Individuals, or even departments, have their own objectives which take precedence in their own minds over the organization's. Lecturers who devote their time almost exclusively to their own research as a means of advancing their careers convince themselves that research is far more important than teaching. Likewise, those who take on lucrative consultancy contracts rather than carry out genuine research, will be sure that they are performing a socially more worthwhile task. The formal goals of an organization are often not achieved in practice. To some extent, this happens when individual and even departmental goals are pursued to the exclusion of the formal goal. But the formal goal may be unrealistic, or the environment may alter to make its achievement more difficult. When any of these happen, we find that the final product of the organization was unintended. This has been called a *real* goal. For example, when a school in a deprived area, intending formally to pursue some educational goal seems for whatever reason, to perform the social function of keeping children off the streets during the day, it can be said that its 'real' goal is custodial rather than educational. More accurately, however, this 'real' goal is better described as an indication of the school's low level of effectiveness. Similarly, a university and its teachers may be intending to produce the managing directors of tomorrow. Empirical investigation may demonstrate, however, that they are in fact producing the foremen, the personnel assistants, the technicians, the secretaries and nurses of today.

As well as operating at different levels in an organization, goals are also of different kinds. We wish to distinguish three main kinds here. The first is what we call *end-product* or *output goals*. This refers to what the organization produces. In the case of the university this will be graduates and new knowledge. It is important, however, to distinguish between different kinds of product, different types of graduate, different types of knowledge. This we call the *quality/characteristics goal*. Thus the Robbins Committee sought graduates who were "cultivated men and women". Some technological universities appear more concerned with giving graduates a close appreciation of practical matters. Similarly, some will follow 'pure' research, others more 'useful' knowledge. Some business schools seek to produce 'hard-nosed' quantitive methods men, others prefer an orientation towards human relations skills. Thirdly, there are the goals which are generated from within the organization itself. These are usually referred to as the *system* or *system maintenance goals*. These can often be more important than output or quality goals. There will be pressure from within the organizational system itself towards growth or perhaps stability, to resist changes or to be continuously innovating. The system goals also deal with the 'how' aspect of universities. How does it try to accommodate its students? In halls of residence, in supervised flats, in approved lodgings, or does it consider this is something to leave to the free market and free choice of the student?

Goals, then, are not simple concepts. One cannot state the aim of the university in one or two sentences and expect to say something meaningful. The different kinds of goals, and the way in which they operate at different levels must be considered if a formulation of goals is to provide a guide to action.

Against this background, let us consider some recent or classical statements about university goals. "The university is an institution designed for the advancement and dissemination of knowledge. The purpose of the university is to benefit the community which created and maintains it, and mankind in general, through the advancement and dissemination of knowledge." (J. Searle: *The Campus War,* Penguin, 1972, p. 170.)

"The university ideal, which derives from the corporation of masters and scholars of the middle ages, is of a self-governing community concerned with advancing and disseminating knowledge." (A. E. Sloman: *The Making of a University,* BBC, 1964, p. 9.)

"A university is a corporation or society which devotes itself to a search after knowledge for the sake of its intrinsic value." (B. Truscot: *Redbrick University,* Faber, 1943, p. 45.)

"I shall treat a university as though it had two major subsystems: one for the discovery of knowledge—research; the other for the dissemination of knowledge—teaching." (A. K. Rice: *The Modern University,* Tavistock, 1970, p. 24.)

"There would be widespread agreement with the view that the fundamental characteristic is the combination of research with teaching." (G. L. Brook: *The Modern University,* Deutsch, 1965, p. 11.)

All of these assertions are entirely prescriptive, although only Dr. Sloman's is avowedly so, and give no indication of how these objects may be achieved or any indication of how we may determine when these objects are being followed and when they are not. There is no apparent concern for what occurs in practice. One fears, indeed, that many vice-chancellors of British universities, if asked the goal of their institution, would be unable to give a more informative reply. One possible answer has come from the American administrator/academic, Jacques Barzun that "the universities are expected, among other things, to turn out scientists and engineers, foster international understanding, provide a home for the arts, satisfy divergent tasks in culture and sexual morals, cure cancer, recast the penal code and train equally for the professions and for a life of cultured contentment in the Coming Era of Leisure".[16]

In other words, as universities in the twentieth century have grown, countless new functions have been grafted on with little regard for how this growth of one function will affect the operation of others. We have seen the scramble for funds for management and business education among British universities in the sixties and seventies. Similarly, we can observe the passion with which several universities compete with each other for the acquisition of a new medical school without any apparent regard for the effect the inclusion of a medical school will have on their institution, without considering what present deficiency in the university's make-up makes it essential to acquire a medical school. But the value of a medical school, or a business school, is like the advancement of knowledge, a revealed truth, not to be questioned.

There is nothing in the statements of university goals which we have examined to help us in answering questions about university development. There is always the gulf that exists between the formal, prescriptive aims and reality. To illustrate this we may turn to the oft-quoted goals set down by the Robbins Committee. The first Robbins goal was that of "training in useful skills" in order that graduates could play a part in society's division of labour. This is one of the university's oldest goals. Traditionally, universities prepared students for the church and for teaching, and in Scotland and Europe, for medicine and the law as well. As Roger Ascham put it in the sixteenth century, "I know that universities be instituted only that the realm be served with preachers, lawyers and physicians."[17] Arguably, the traditional outlets are still well served by the universities. Any deficiencies in the education offered to the potential lawyer or physician usually result from formal requirements of professional bodies, to whose needs the universities perhaps too readily respond.

It is doubtful, however, if the same can be said of the relationship of university education to a career in industry and commerce. While newer social sciences like psychology and sociology are supplying the social services with welcomed recruits, there is widespread unease in industry about the employability of those trained in the physical sciences. To industry, such graduates often appear over-specialized, and find adaptation to industry difficult. The university response to criticism has been to defend the specialized nature of science training, especially the pure research Ph.D. degree, and to create more widely based courses only for the second rate. In the social sciences, the same tendency is to be found, although to a lesser extent. In England, in particular, the pressure in recent years is to specialize in one discipline only, at a time when the disciplines themselves develop into ritualized mystiques, more and more remote from reality. This can be exemplified by those economists who seek intellectual respectability by retreating into mathematics, which to those actually concerned with pricing and investment policies, seems an exercise in the highest nonsense. In these cases we see a clear clash between the 'vocational training' and the 'advancement of knowledge' goals. Research in pure science means staff becoming more and specialized in their interests, to the extent that one teacher can allege that for some of his colleagues "lectures consist almost entirely of the often tedious details of their own research, and other equally important parts of the syllabus are treated superficially, if at all".[18] At the same time, the social sciences seek some kind of academic respectability by becoming either more quantitative or by attempting to become more abstract.

The goal of 'advancement of learning' is one output goal of universities about which there is little dispute. It is generally accepted that universities should be concerned with discovery, and that much of a university's resources should be devoted to this end. The unanimity about this goal is seen to disappear, however, if we cease to regard it as an output goal and view it from the perspective of quality/characteristics. In one view the mission of the university is the pursuit of knowledge for its own sake. "Not 'relevant' knowledge; not 'practical' knowledge; not the kind of knowledge that enables one to wield power, achieve success, or influence others", as Robert Nisbet has put it.[19] To several vice-chancellors of British universities the opposite appears to be the case. Brunel and Bradford, to name but two, see both teaching and research work largely in terms of their 'usefulness' to society.

The dispute between the government and the research councils over the funding of science research can be seen in quality/ characteristic terms. The government, following a recommendation of the Downing St. Central Policy Review Staff headed by Lord Rothschild, wishes to encourage government departments increasingly to make their own arrangements with individual universities about research relevant to their needs, and to take away corresponding amounts from the research councils. The government's case is that this will speed a necessary transfer of resources from 'basic' research towards more 'user-oriented' programmes. In medicine and agriculture, particularly, it will give greatly increased power to the relevant government departments, whilst virtually emasculating these two research councils. Whatever the validity of either view, it is apparent that the mere assertion of 'advancement of knowledge' does not help much in trying to understand what a university is attempting to achieve and by what measure its performance can be judged. We have to be more specific in order to be aware that 'teaching and research' are not always inextricably interlinked, but that the service of one goal may clash with the achievement of the other, and that awareness of a 'research' goal can be meaningful only if viewed from the quality/characteristic angle.

If we examine the remaining two of the Robbins Committee's goals, it is readily apparent that frequently neither goal is actually achieved. One of them was that what is taught should be taught in such a way as to promote the general powers of the mind. The aim, the Committee suggested, was to produce not mere specialists, but cultivated men and women. They suggested that even if something practical was being taught it should be taught at a level of generality which allows the application of these techniques to many problems. This has been dismissed by some as an aim honoured more in the breach than in the observance. It might be held that much technical instruction simply cannot be carried out at a high level of generalization. It might also be held that the Committee is reflecting only a new version of the belief that a good 'classical' education befits a man to tackle any intellectual problem he is likely to encounter. Again, however, there is no hint whatsoever of *how* this aim is to be achieved. The aim itself has interesting possibilities as a test for deciding which subjects and courses are fit for study at university level. Either as a test, or as a goal for an existing course, systematic attention is required as to how such a goal can be implemented.

The last goal mentioned by the Robbins Committee, the idea of the university transmitting a common culture and common standards of citizenship, has probably attracted most scorn. Manifestly, it is a goal hardly even aspired to, outside a handful of smaller or collegiate universities, and it is a notion almost unheard of in the large 'civic' universities. Yet the idea that universities have wider aims than simply developing intellectual interests, a technical expertise, that they have some concern with the quality of life, is far from absent in discussing the universities' function in society. The Committee itself admitted that they found difficulty in conveying the meaning of the concept they were concerned to explain. They might have been better understood had they attempted to indicate how it could be achieved.

If a goal is genuinely desired, then some kind of programme for action has to be laid down. The *means* necessary to achieving the goal have to be identified and obtained. Some standard of achievement has to be established and, however crudely, some attempt has to be made to measure the degree of success obtained, i.e. the relative effectiveness of the programme.

There is obviously scope for debate about what the purposes of a university should be in Great Britain at the present time. We have noted in the previous chapter the variety of university institutions in the country. It would be surprising if there was total unanimity of purpose among them. Yet statements of university goals are still made as if they applied to all equally. There may be wide agreement that universities have a commitment to research and to education. It may be agreed also that education includes both the transmission of skills and some sense of personal development of the student. But the emphasis to be placed on each of these aims will vary, as will the interpretation of what is meant by them. To understand what a university is trying to achieve, its formal aims will have to be set out in what we have called output and quality/characteristic terms.

Let it not be assumed that Glasgow University, 67 per cent of whose students live at home, is doing the same as Cambridge with its collegiate structure, nor let us pretend, either, that it is doing the same as Brunel with its strong 'sandwich' course element (i.e. half of the students' time spent in industry, half in the university). Because most of its students live at home, this does not mean that Glasgow University need not have a 'social' goal of the kind a residential university would have. It does suggest, however, that the means adopted to effect it would have to be very different.

So, too, with course-work. It is not enough to intone piously that teaching should promote the general powers of the mind. They have to be promoted actively. It means revising courses, rethinking teaching methods, assessing performance, and most important of all, rewarding performance. This applies to students who will get worthwhile degrees and to teachers who may expect status and financial advancement. It may even mean interfering with the treasured autonomy of the university teacher in the classroom to teach what he likes and how he likes, as some interpret 'academic freedom'. It probably means that courses should be devised, taught and assessed by tightly-knit teams rather than by a series of individuals—much in the way that most of the Open University's courses have been developed. We have to be concerned as much with the methods used as with the overall stated aim.

What we have, in fact, is a management problem. The overall process in implementing a new course is not essentially different from launching a new product. Objectives are set, plans are made, personnel selected, resources allocated, and production gets under way. Often in universities the process then stops. There should, however, be a further phase, control of the output. As in any management programme, attention also has to be given to motivating staff and to evaluating performance. This is but one example of how usefully a management process could work in the university. This same goal-oriented approach can also be applied to specialist courses, although the need for control is probably less, and also to research work. In approaching the university's activities systematically in relation to the output or quality/characteristic goals sought, anomalies and downright contradictions can be detected. It may not be possible, for example, to provide professional or vocational training in a course which also seeks to provide students with a strong theoretical or intellectual underpinning. One frequently finds this tension in engineering departments. A current example is the division which appears to have arisen between the sociological theorists and the social administration teachers at the London School of Economics.

In terms of quality/characteristic goals, it is futile to try to implement less specialized degree courses alongside the specialized ones, when the reward structure of the university is geared to advancing the specialized researcher. In this case, the two possible quality goals appear irreconcilable until the systems goals are changed also. Esteem and rewards have to be given in a meaningful and tangible way to performance and success in teaching broader and even inter-disciplinary degree work. Similar recognition has to be given to students who take broader or joint degrees in terms of their eligibility to receive research grants and appointments. If the systems goals are not altered consciously in this way, then the institution should not even try to change its quality goals, since the change is doomed to failure. It is because many attempts at change in universities founder that we advocate this conscious goal-orientation. British universities have not suffered to the same extent from random unplanned growth as have many American institutions. Nevertheless, the problem exists, the self-doubt exists, and one way to resolve it is through a conscious goal-setting operation.

Now, some readers *au fait* with management fads may be alarmed that we are addicted to the currently fashionable cult of 'Management by Objectives' (M.b.O.) or 'Management by Results'. Be reassured! If an organizational analyst has any 'message' it is a simple one: "Beware of management panaceas!" Alas, M.b.O., first indicated by Peter Drucker[20] in 1955, and developed by Douglas McGregor and others in the late 1950s,[21] as a new approach to motivating and controlling industrial managers, and converted by John Humble[22] and imitators into a lucrative consultants' package, now deserves that description.

There is a danger, at a time when there are many pressures on universities to be more 'management conscious', that they may try to introduce some variant of M.b.O. What this chapter has been at pains to point out is the importance of goals at the planning stage, of the different kinds of goals that can exist, of the different levels at which they operate, of the complexities of the links between different kinds of goals. M.b.O. is more concerned with goals or targets as motivators of personnel (since, when it is done properly, staff largely set their own goals) and as a means of organizational control that takes the emphasis away from procedures and towards end-results.

In universities, concentration upon end-results with no attention being paid to how the results are achieved is clearly inadvisable. The manner in which teaching or research is carried out is important. In research it is often possible for a teacher to take credit for work which really represents the tears, sweat and skills of his research students. Similarly, in teaching, the high motivation and ability of students frequently lead to good end-results in terms of examination success, despite lack of preparation, interest and sometimes even presence on the part of the lecturer.

Nevertheless, if universities are to make use of the concept of organizational effectiveness, some means must be discovered of assessing performance. At present, measurement of a kind exists. It takes the form of counting the number of articles published. Quality of work is rarely taken into account, since assessment of research activity in highly specialized areas is not easy. Also, the value placed upon research work depends upon what the reviewer considers important. Is it theoretical refinement, rigorous methodology, applicability of the results, or what? A deliberate attempt to establish apt criteria which are collectively acceptable to those whose performance is being reviewed is preferable to no attempt being made at all.

In science, a number of possible measures of performance have been developed by social scientists investigating those factors which improve or impair scientific performance. For example, Peltz and Andrews, in a study[23] of 1,300 American scientists, adopted an admittedly crude measure based on both 'objective' and 'subjective' factors. The 'objective' approach was simply to count the publications, patents, and reports produced by scientists over the previous five years. This was qualified, however, by an 'internal' report from each laboratory where each scientist was asked to provide a ranking order (1-n) for all the other people in the laboratory he felt competent to judge. He was asked to make two separate rankings, the first on the contribution of each man to his field of knowledge within the past five years, the second ranking upon each man's overall usefulness in helping the unit to carry out its responsibilities. A variation of this kind of method could probably be adapted for universities.

In teaching, assessment is likely to pose greater problems. If, however, teaching excellence is to be rewarded, as virtually everyone agrees it should be, these problems will have to be faced. When Mr. Aubrey Jones, as chairman of the Prices and Incomes Board, suggested in 1968 that 'merit' awards be given to those with heavy teaching commitments or to those whose teaching was outstanding, he cautiously suggested that part of the assessment could include rating by consumers, namely students. Such was the furore that this P.I.B. suggestion was promptly rejected by the government. In the event, 'merit' awards for exceptional teaching were, despite the hostility of the profession, awarded, usually on the recommendation of heads of departments. It goes without saying that heads of departments made assessments of their subordinates' teaching capacities, but what the criteria for these assessments were must remain one of the mysteries of our time.

The foregoing discussion has, of course, only been about the formal goals of a university, viewed in terms of the final output, and, to some extent, in terms of its quality/characteristics. Little has been said about the goals of the individual members of the university, or about those objectives generated by the organization itself, which we referred to earlier as system-maintenance goals.

Every individual member of a university, be he professor, administrator, lecturer, graduate, undergraduate, librarian, or whatever, has his own desires and aspirations which he hopes the university will satisfy to some degree. Obviously, how the individuals who make up the university see its goals in relation to their own is important. Clearly, it is impossible to ascertain the perceptions and goals of every individual in a university. Even if it were possible, one could come to no meaningful conclusion unless these views were organized into certain broad categories, as we attempt to do in a later chapter.

c

We should be aware, however, that a university as a whole generates goals which derive from the needs of the ongoing organization. One outstanding example in recent years of such a system goal is growth. Expansion, especially into new ventures, brings a greater power and status to those who control universities. It brings greater career opportunities to all academics and administrators alike. Once the advantages of growth become apparent, almost every group in the university soon comes to have a vested interest in continued growth for growth's sake. The slowing-down of university expansion in the quinquennium 1972–77 may well be criticized on academic grounds (i.e. in terms of output and quality goals), but a great deal of university fury may result from the effect that restricted expansion may have upon the 'system' goals of all universities.

In addition, the needs of particular sub-groups lead to the emergence of a variety of system-maintenance sub-goals. One such example could be students' associations. The existence of student grievances may lead to the provision, constitutional or otherwise, of a settlement procedure. Because, however, of the existence of students who seek office in students' organizations, the use of constitutional procedure becomes an important means of indicating their usefulness to their electorate. Increased influence for student representatives on various university bodies—from departmental committees to the governing bodies —becomes a means of justifying the existence and of extending the scope of student associations or unions. In other words, this machinery will be used, not necessarily because student opinion or insight may be of particular value in a given situation, but because the student association has an in-built bias towards seeking consultation and extending its influence. Not necessarily because the university needs this to happen, not necessarily because the student body needs it, but because the student association needs it.

Similarly, an increased sophistication in the university administrative procedure is a system goal of university administrators. It is in their overall professional interest if more resources are devoted to the 'management' function of universities, if more specialized professional skills come to be necessary to practise the art of administration. Where the administrative function is at the 'penny-farthing' stage, an amalgam of elementary book-keeping, clerical and secretarial skills, to which any academic can turn his attention at a day's notice—and this is the traditional model of administration in universities—then the status and influence of one whose full-time occupation is administration is bound to be low. The administrator has a vested interest in making his skills non-transferable. Complicated procedures which few can understand, budgetary devices and accounting techniques which academics frequently have neither the time nor the skills to unravel can be a systems goal of the administrative cadres. We do not suggest that this is the only reason why university administration is a great deal more complicated now than it was ten years ago. But it would be foolish to deny the simple truth that the professional administrator has benefited from this process and has a vested interest in seeing it continue.

As far as academic staff are concerned, they too have a variety of system goals. By far the most important is the concept of academic freedom. One reason, however, why 'academic freedom' is a magical rallying cry in university circles is the unsurprising one that the term means different things to different people. At least three common meanings can be found in contemporary usage. These are, first of all, freedom of the individual teacher, which means, on the one hand, freedom from arbitrary discrimination on the grounds of religion, sex, race or politics, and, on the other hand, freedom to pursue research which only he chooses and to teach his subject in the way that he chooses. Secondly, the term is used to refer to the autonomy of the university as an institution. In contemporary terms, this effectively means freedom from government intervention in policy matters, but it could also refer to religious bodies and industry. Thirdly, the term is used to refer to academic self-government, i.e. that the control of the universities should be in the hands of academics and that these academics should to a large extent be representative of the academic community as a whole.

Some awareness of each of these three aspects of this notion of academic freedom is essential if one is to make sense of the value system of university teachers, or to understand some of the controversies in the governing of universities, or to follow the nuances of the relationships between universities and governments. Each aspect of academic freedom does not apply with equal emphasis to all groups of university members. Most teachers will be concerned primarily with the individual aspect, to a lesser degree with notions of academic democracy, and usually more remotely with their university's relations with external bodies. Administrators will have a different scale of priorities and academics of different rank may well interpret the balance of alternatives in different ways.

The tradition of individual freedom seems to derive largely from the success of the nineteenth century German universities which caused their major features to be admired and copied in the English-speaking world, particularly in the United States. The fundamental teaching principle was that the professor had freedom to teach and research what and how he pleased (*Lehrfreiheit*), balanced by the student's freedom to study where he liked and to work at his own pace (*Lernfreiheit*). As perhaps may be observed, such an apparently anarchic procedure could work only within a predominantly conservative and authoritarian culture, such as nineteenth century Prussia. Taken up and adapted by those American universities whose academic leaders admired the research-orientation of the German model, the concept gradually extended to embrace the lesser creatures of the academic world. Basically, however, the argument depended upon the teacher being an authority in his chosen field, whose knowledge and wisdom none could dare to question or judge. This idea has become embodied in the mythology of science, where the notion of the autonomy of the researcher as an essential functional requirement of research activity has assumed the status of a sacred truth. Despite some recent evidence that questions the concept's relevance for contemporary scientific research, there is certainly a strong case to be made for this approach to research, and more importantly, it is an important component in the value system of university scientists.

The contemporary importance of this value is, however, not confined only to research or to scientists. It is held to be important in the classroom as well as in the laboratory, and it is considered an essential precondition for scholarly enquiry in any field. The Robbins Committee, for example, did not question the basic relevance of the concept. They recognized that this individual freedom, combined with security of tenure, was open to abuse. They remarked that the danger of such abuse was much less than the danger of trying to eliminate it by general restriction of individual liberty.[24]

One incident frequently quoted as an example of the violation of this principle was the dismissal in 1969 of two lecturers at the London School of Economics. One of these was Mr. Robin Blackburn, who was sacked for allegedly condoning and encouraging the use of violence by students of the School in pulling down gates recently installed by the authorities. It has been claimed that Mr. Blackburn was victimized for holding opinions uncongenial to those of the School authorities. According to this view of individual freedom, provided that Mr. Blackburn's competence as a sociologist was not in question, he had an undisputed right to continued employment. It should be noted, however, that the whole concept has always been concerned with the integrity of the individual teacher to his subject. If Blackburn's sociology had been unconventional or unpopular with the authorities and he were dismissed for that, then none would doubt that academic freedom was being infringed. As it was, however, Blackburn's alleged actions had nothing to do with his being a sociologist, and his dismissal was the result of his alleged failure to observe his obligations as a member of the academic community or as an employee, as the authorities perceived them. He may or may not have been wrongfully dismissed, but his individual academic freedom as a sociologist was not infringed.

Another celebrated case, that of Dr. David Craig in 1972 at Lancaster University, is much more complicated. In this case, the dispute arose from the judgement of the Head of the English Department at Lancaster University that Dr. Craig's teaching had undue political undertones and that his marking was biased. Dr. Craig, of course, disputed this view, and, for several reasons, objected to his transfer to other teaching commitments. The students in the department supported Dr. Craig's position, went on strike and successfully persuaded many others to join them. The Vice-Chancellor accused Dr. Craig of inciting the students to disrupt the university and sought to dismiss him. Dr. Craig denied the charges, claiming that he had merely supplied the students with information about the dispute in the department when asked for it. Eventually Dr. Craig was not dismissed, but transferred to other teaching duties in the university. As far as the dispute within the English Department was concerned, there appears to have been a clash between the principle of Dr. Craig's individual freedom, and the right, and indeed the duty, of a Head of Department to ensure that duties within his department are properly performed. In passing, we might observe that the Robbins Committee had noted[25] that, although the realization of freedom within the individual department could bring considerable difficulties in detail, there was no great difficulty in the general principle. As the Craig case illustrates, however, it is impossible to reconcile the tradition of individual academic freedom with the principle of hierarchy in the organization of university departments.

The second meaning of the academic freedom we have identified refers to the freedom of the university from interference in its affairs by any external body. One feature which distinguishes universities from other institutions of higher education in Britain today is that there is no direct link between central or local government and the governing bodies of universities. For this reason, universities and some related institutions are referred to as the 'autonomous' sector of higher education. This position contrasts with the universities of Europe and with the public or State universities of the United States, where control is ultimately in the hands of central or state governments.

Like most American 'private' universities, with which some parallel can be drawn, British universities are dependent upon public funds for survival. In Britain, the degree of dependence upon the central government is almost total. The universities have in recent years come under increasing pressure that they be more accountable for their expenditure of public monies. We do not ask here, "Why should universities remain free of public control?", but we do note that, historically, establishing their own autonomy, either from civic or ecclesiastical authorities, has been a major system goal of universities since medieval times.

The third aspect of academic freedom, that the government of universities shall be in the hands of academics has its origin in the history of the two ancient English universities. There, the basic unit of organization has always been the college. Until very recently the 'universities' of Oxford and Cambridge were virtually only examining and degree-awarding bodies. Countless tales are recounted of itinerant scholars and tourists who have long trudged the back streets of Oxford and Cambridge in a vain search for 'the University'. Both within the semi-autonomous colleges where all fellows were equal, and upon the relatively rare occasions when the universities' 'governing bodies' had to make or ratify decisions, all academics had equal voice.

The Oxbridge experience means that there exists a tradition that all scholars have equal rights in ratifying decisions. By contrast, almost all the later universities of England and Wales have followed the Scottish/Continental model of hierarchical academic organization based upon the department rather than the college. In most cases final decisions or ratification of decisions are taken by governing bodies in which academic representatives are heavily outnumbered by 'lay' representatives. The existence of the Oxford and Cambridge tradition has meant that there has been a constant state of latent tension between the formal administrative arrangements of the 'civic' university and the value system of the academic staff, many of whom had experienced collegiate organization as students or as teachers.

These three aspects of 'academic freedom' are basic to any understanding of the process of academic activity and government within universities. Some aspects of the concept often appear bewildering to anyone accustomed to the norms of behaviour of the industrial and commercial world. Businessmen, for instance, have expressed amazement at the near impossibility of dismissing academic staff unless, to quote Strathclyde's charter, which is fairly typical, they commit any act of an "immoral, scandalous or disgraceful nature", or can be proven to suffer from such a "gross physical or mental disability" that makes them unfit to perform their duties. One can be fired for sleeping with students, or for being drunk and disorderly, but not for idleness. Bizarre or not, 'academic freedom' is a major reference point for behaviour or actions within the 'closed system' of the university world.

Our task in this chapter has not been to find a statement of university goals which applies to all British universities. We have noted that there is substantial agreement that universities are about research and about education, but that interpretations of what these mean for particular institutions can vary widely, both in terms of what we have called the output and quality/ characteristics. Moreover, from within the organization itself, goals emerge that are important to its continued successful functioning. We have suggested that not only should the complexity and variety of goals be known and understood, but also that a conscious goal-oriented analysis be applied to most university activities. In this way, considerations of organizational effectiveness may outweigh those of simple efficiency in university decision-making.

CHAPTER 3

Structure of Government

In any organization, once goals have been established, the next
step is to organize resources in order that the organization
may work towards achieving its ends. Different jobs are allocated
to different people. Whether "one" is organizing a grocer's shop
or a tennis club, responsibilities are divided up. This may be
done very informally at the grocer's, but even at the tennis
club, jobs will have different titles. President, vice-president,
secretary, treasurer, social convener, these and other titles
indicate the different functions performed by the persons filling
these positions. Our point, in brief, is that the process of division
of labour is basic to the notion of organization. Specialization
of task is found in any group of human beings which is formally
organized, be it a primitive tribe, multi-national corporation,
or a university.

It is customary to approach the concept of organization-
structure from the activity or task to be carried out. The process
of organization involves breaking this overall task into more
manageable sub-tasks and allocating these to separate individuals
who, in turn, may break their own tasks down still further
and allocate work to another subordinate layer. This division
of tasks is accompanied by a devolution of authority to the
various managers to ensure that their tasks are carried out,
and they are then held responsible for ensuring that their contribution to the overall task of the enterprise is carried out.
These relationships—how tasks are divided, how authority is
allocated, and how responsibility is divided—are often depicted
on organization charts. This formal distribution of tasks and
responsibilities is the starting point for any analysis examining

[Handwritten marginal notes: "By whom? for whom? A – hystorical myth?" "The point is – who is doing, the organizing, who is being organized?" "yes – but such specialization is not the result only of technical constraints. It is also a form of social organization."]

the way in which work is carried out. For too many analyses it is also the finishing point, which is a serious error, but the authority structure is the base upon which every organization is built.

In terms of structure, there is considerable variety in the detailed constitutional arrangements embodied in the Charters or Statutes of individual universities. Several broad categories can, however, be easily identified and, with a few exceptions, common patterns of organization can be established. The major exceptions, paradoxical considering their influence in the recent history of British higher education, are the ancient English universities of Oxford and Cambridge. Their administrative arrangements, and these are remarkably similar, are entirely different from those of every other university institution in Britain. For this reason, none of the immediately following generalizations apply to them. Apart, perhaps, from the University of London, distinctions rather than exceptions have to be made from a broadly similar structure which is common to all the universities of Britain. Although the University of Wales is usually considered, like London, as a federal university with a mainly examining and degree-awarding function, nearly all its constituent colleges have themselves an internal structure little different from that of an independent university.

The most common pattern found is that which we will call the English civic model. This model of government was developed in the nineteenth century in the provincial universities of England, such as Birmingham, Manchester, Leeds, Liverpool and Bristol which, today, despite their apparent lack of attraction to the media, are the backbone of the higher education system of the country. The main feature of this model is that of government by committee. The topmost tier in this hierarchy of committees is a supreme governing body called the Court. In all cases, this is a large and unwieldy body, formed originally to give an articulation of local interest in a university, but which nowadays has no importance in decision-making. In the main, it is composed of representatives of academic staff and graduates, nominees of other universities, local authorities, religious denominations, professional bodies, and so on. Size varies considerably, but no university has a court of less than a hundred members. The Robbins Committee reported a variation from Manchester with 129 to Sheffield with 605. The main function of the Court nowadays is to meet once or twice a year to review the accounts and hear reports from the university. Its main duty is to elect the Chancellor, the ceremonial head of the university, whose function is mainly symbolic. It is frequently suggested that the Court has outlived its usefulness. Durham abolished its Court some ten years ago, without consequent calamity, and Birmingham's recent Review Body has recommended that its Court should be ceremonial only. At Sussex, the Court's powers are limited to appointing the Chancellor and Pro-Chancellors, the Treasurer and a number of representatives to Council, and to discussing the annual report and accounts. Similarly, the nearest equivalent Scottish body, the General Council, has no formal authority.

The most important body, in terms of formal powers, is the Council. Since this is the body responsible for the finances of the university, it has the major policy-making powers. It usually appoints the Vice-Chancellor in consultation with the Senate. The Council is also the body which formally makes academic appointments and these have to be both authorized and approved by it. In effect, academic appointments are made by academics, but this formal requirement of Council approval, together with the need in some universities for the Council to approve academic regulations as well, has irked some academic spokesmen. The resentment is caused primarily by the fact that in most Councils the academic members are outnumbered by external or 'lay' members by something like four to one. It is a much smaller body than the Court and is able to act with some degree of effectiveness. The Robbins Report quoted Sheffield's Council as being the largest, with 45 members. Manchester's was the smallest with 29, while Birmingham, Exeter, Leicester and Sussex, all had 34. In addition to these members, there is usually provision for co-option. Most of the academic members are professors. They outnumber non-professorial representatives by a ratio of at least 2:1. Usually the academic members are elected by the Senate.

The Council can be styled the effective governing body of the civic university, and its influence is felt in every area of university activity. In practice, as well as in theory, in most places it avoids involving itself in purely academic matters and rarely, if ever, conflicts with the Senate. Nevertheless, because of its financial control, it does have great influence over the shape of academic development. It is the Council that decides upon which buildings and accommodation have priority, how many academic posts will exist, and the allocation of resources between academic and non-academic purposes. Because of its power, the Council has come under criticism from academic staff for two main reasons. The first is that such a powerful body as this should have a predominantly 'lay' membership. Decisions which affect the university should be made only by those who are involved in the consequences of these decisions, and who, more importantly, have sufficient knowledge and understanding of how the university works to make the right decisions. This means that effective decision-making should be in the hands of academic staff. Secondly, whilst professors are to some extent represented upon councils, non-professorial staff have, in all but a few cases, little more than nominal representation.

It is argued that, as with the Court, university Councils have outlived their usefulness. Where local interests contributed a large proportion of a university's finance, and where universities had a mainly local orientation and drew students primarily from the surrounding districts, as was the case in the nineteenth century, local representation and control on governing bodies made some sense. Nowadays, however, local interests contribute proportionately very little to a university's budget, the great bulk of finance coming from the central government via the University Grants Committee; the overall orientation of most universities is national or international, and very few students at any one university come from its immediate vicinity. Thus the case for local control is hardly a strong one.

The Robbins Committee, however, made great play of the 'watchdog' role of the 'lay' member. The presence on governing bodies of universities of respected public figures was an assurance to the populace at large that public funds were being spent in a proper manner. This argument, however, failed to impress the House of Commons Public Accounts Committee which, since the early fifties, has argued that university finances be opened to public scrutiny, i.e. by their own official, the Comptroller and Auditor General. The logic of this argument was finally accepted in 1967 by the then Secretary of State for Education, and since 1970 the accounts of the U.G.C. and of individual universities have been scrutinized by the Comptroller's staff. With this development, the 'watchdog' role of the lay members seems to have disappeared. The argument now rests upon the value to the university of having men of affairs, not only giving advice upon the 'business' side of a university's operations, but also publicly identifying with and helping to foster an image of the university being alive to the needs and interests of the wider society. A less laudable function has also been suggested, that of powerful 'lay' members being able to attract funds from private donors, both for general university purposes and for sponsoring research.

(3) Next in importance in the university's structure of government is the university's main academic body, the Senate. This is the body responsible for the teaching and disciplining of students. Heads of departments are usually accountable to the Senate for the performance of their departments' teaching and research duties. Matters such as admissions are usually delegated to boards of faculties or schools or to departments, but the Senate remains responsible for this and other work which it delegates to lower levels in the organization. The Senate is traditionally composed of all the professors of the university, *ex officio,* plus a limited number of representatives of the non-professorial staff, plus a few administrative figures such as the registrar and the librarian. This traditional composition, especially since during the past decade most universities have increased the number of elected non-professorial representatives to between a quarter and a third of the *ex officio* members, has meant that Senates have become large unwieldy bodies quite incapable of any decision-making facility. The bulk of the work of such large Senates (e.g. Manchester's with two hundred and eighty members) is farmed out to committees, who take the effective decisions which the full Senate usually ratifies in due course, although not always without protracted discussion. The Vice-Chancellor is chairman of Senate and this is the source of the power Vice-Chancellors wield.

Where the composition of Senate follows these traditional lines, and this is still by far the most common practice, the size of the Senate varies with the size of the university. Even in smaller institutions this can mean a Senate of more than fifty members. A number of universities have in recent years experimented with ending automatic Senate membership for professors, in an attempt to reduce the size of Senates and to restore to that body an effective decision-making function. Some recent reforms of the Senates of the older English civic universities have been more concerned with making them more representative or democratic, rather than with transforming them into more effective decision-making bodies. Leeds University, in 1973, ended the automatic right of all professors to a Senate seat. Heads of departments, however, will retain this right and the 45 professors who lose their seats will be replaced by an additional 41 elected non-professorial staff and seven student members. The new Senate, operating from 1974, will have 74 heads of departments, 45 elected members, 15 *ex officio* members, 7 students and up to 7 co-opted members, i.e. 158 members as against the 120 (with only 4 elected non-professors). Leeds, therefore, might be said to be only catching up with universities such as Liverpool and Manchester which have increased the proportion of elected non-professorial senators from, in the case of Manchester, nil in 1963, to 25 per cent.

The former colleges of advanced technology have been more radical. In few have professors automatic right to representation and the overall composition of some, like Aston, Brunel and City, makes it likely that they will not exceed 30–40. The secret of small Senates is basically to have professors elected, either on a school or faculty basis, by their fellow professors, or by all staff, with a similar franchise applying to a fixed proportion of elected non-professors.

Beneath the Senate, the next unit of organization is, in all but a few cases, the department. Most departments have an appointed head, traditionally 'the professor', or holder of a specific chair. Where there is more than one chair in a department, there may be some election by the professors to the chairmanship, or the headship may rotate. The department is the point at which the real business of the university is carried out. The critical position is that of full professor, or head of department. The teaching and research staff will almost invariably be responsible to him for the fulfilment of their duties. To gain advancement or to be promoted, his favour is essential.

In all departments, but most especially those science and technology departments in which research work depends upon acquisition of, access to, and use of, expensive and complex equipment, those who are not in favour, it has been said, find their work and careers jeopardized. The professor, in turn, is usually responsible to the Senate or to the Council for the performance of his duties, which usually means to no one. In effect, the Vice-Chancellor, as chairman of Senate, and because he, in his turn, can wield substantial power in terms of his influence over the distribution of resources, acts as the only check upon professors' performances, if he has the inclination, time or energy.

Between Senate and department there is usually interposed on organization charts of universities, the faculties, as they are known in the older universities, or schools, as in the newer. These are usually a means of co-ordinating departments whose work is closely related, or who may share students with one another. The groupings vary from one university to another. In some, the faculty of arts may include, as well as traditional arts subjects such as languages and philosophy, social sciences and business or management studies. Another university may separate these into different faculties or schools, of arts, of social sciences, and of commerce or business. Similarly, there may be one faculty of engineering or several. These are essentially co-ordinative bodies. Such powers as they may have will have been specifically delegated to them by the Senate. In recent years, the importance of faculties has tended to increase because of the difficulties large Senates have experienced in trying to legislate and administer the academic affairs of the university. Not only have more powers been devolved, but also, Senates increasingly insist that any new proposals from departments must first be discussed in the boards of faculties and must only come before the Senate as a recommendation from the faculty. This gives many faculties an important effective right of veto. Because faculty boards are usually composed of professors *ex officio* plus some elected non-professors, internal discussion within a department can be publicly aired and this can, therefore, be an important level in the decision process to the non-professorial academic staff.

However, before we examine the interrelationship of the

powers of the various layers in universities' structures of government, we must mention those universities whose structures do
not correspond in detail with the above description of the
English civic university. In order of difference from the model,
these are the University of Wales, the Scottish universities, the
University of London, and the Universities of Oxford and
Cambridge.

The University of Wales is often given a separate place in
descriptions of the organization of British universities on
account of its federal nature. The constituent colleges of the
University of Wales, however, enjoy substantial autonomy.
Apart from awarding degrees and acting as a post-box through
which government grants are distributed, the University itself
has few effective powers. In terms of organization, each college
operates as a separate unit, and each college, with the exceptions of the Welsh National School of Medicine and the recent
acquisition of St. David's College, Lampeter, has a model of
government approximating to that already outlined.

Next, in order of difference, are the Scottish universities. The
differences are most prominent in the ancient, and still most
important, Universities of St. Andrews, Aberdeen, Glasgow
and Edinburgh. In all of them, however, their supreme governing body is a unit smaller than that of any English Council,
called, confusingly to Englishmen, the Court. At Aberdeen and
at Glasgow, for instance, the Court has only 16 members. It
is chaired by the Rector, who is elected by the students, and
the other members are the Principal, the Lord Provost of the
city, 3 assessors (one each appointed by the Chancellor, the
City council, and the Rector), 6 members elected by the Senate
(including at least 2 non-professors) and 4 by the General
Council. This last body is composed of all the graduates of
the university, plus the academic staff, and while having no
formal powers, could be said to be the ceremonial equivalent
of the English Court.

Thus, although a majority of Court could be said to be 'lay'
members, not only is this a much smaller majority than in
English Councils, but almost all the members have close links
with the university and the General Councils' appointees will
at least be graduates of the university. The four recently chartered
Scottish universities follow this practice in having a similar

Court as the supreme body. For ceremonial and other purposes they also have a body more like an English Court than a General Council. The academic organization of all Scottish universities is, however, similar to the English civic model.

London University, to some extent, is a case apart. By far the largest university in terms of overall student numbers, it is composed of individual colleges which could easily be universities in their own right, such as University, King's or Imperial Colleges, but it also includes separate specialized schools or institutes with a high percentage of postgraduate work. In addition, the London medical schools are associated with the university, although they are organized separately. Overall control of the university is in the hands of a small Court of 17 members; 3 of these are *ex officio,* 6 are appointed by the Senate, 4 by the Crown, 2 by the Inner London Education Authority (I.L.E.A.), plus 2 co-opted members. The Court controls the university's property and finances. It applies for grants to the U.G.C., I.L.E.A. and other public bodies and it allocates the sums received among the various constituent colleges, schools and institutes. There exists also a Senate, supreme in all academic matters, which formally appoints professors and readers in the schools and institutes. The composition of London's Senate differs from all others in that, of its 59 members, only 18 are direct representatives of the teachers, being elected by and from the faculties. Another 18 are graduates, who may, of course, also be teachers elected by the Convocation, composed mainly of the graduates. Beneath the Senate are the boards of faculties and boards of study, with the usual advisory and co-ordinative functions. The above portrayal is, however, somewhat misleading, for the colleges and schools have substantial autonomy. All have a governing body corresponding to the Council of independent English universities, and all have academic boards corresponding in membership and function, though varying greatly in size, to the Senate of independent institutions.

Whilst London, apart from the complication of its medical schools and its tradition of 'recognizing' colleges external to it who prepare students for its degrees, might be held to be different only in degree and variety from the others, the universities of Oxford and Cambridge are entirely different. Their

D

distinguishing features are a total absence of 'lay' participation
or control in their government, and the fact that the basic unit
of organization is overwhelmingly the individual college. The
colleges, are governed democratically by their fellows, i.e. their
teaching staff, admit students and arrange the bulk of teaching.
The university provides lectures and laboratory instruction and
examines the students. University departments arrange the
syllabi of courses, but until recently had no control over the
appointment or teaching capacity of the college fellows who
supervise most of the student's work before his final examinations. With most colleges becoming increasingly dependent upon
U.G.C. funds which are channelled through university bodies,
the central administration has been able to encourage a greater
degree of co-ordination between departments and colleges.
Nevertheless, colleges with substantial endowment income are
able, if they wish, to follow their own inclinations, to a large
extent. The most notorious example of this, of course, has been
All Souls College, Oxford which has resisted the university's
efforts to induce it to admit any students.

The administrative arrangements of Oxford and Cambridge
have not been copied elsewhere. They have, however, provided
a model to which critics of 'lay' influence or of undue professorial power have been able to point as an alternative way
of doing things. This alternative way, such critics can say, despite
its apparent inefficiency and duplication of effort, has not prevented these ancient collegiate universities, for whatever reasons,
from retaining their position as the most prestigious in the
British university system.

Running parallel with these governing arrangements there is
an administration run by full time administrative staff. All of
their work is ultimately the responsibility of Council, Senate,
or of a committee of one of these bodies. Nevertheless, the
day-to-day execution of this work is based usually upon traditional hierarchical lines. In many ways, administrative staff are
the poor relations in the university status systems. Apart from
one or two very senior positions, they are not technically
'members' of the university, unlike even the humblest undergraduate, and have no formal rights of representation in
university government or ceremonies. They are employees,
whether they be cleaners, janitors, accountants, or architects.

The head of this administrative system is the Vice-Chancellor, or Principal in Scotland. He is in the unique position of also being the chief academic officer. Beneath him a registrar or secretary is responsible for the administration. In larger universities there is usually an additional post of bursar, who is responsible directly to the Council for the financial affairs of the university. Beneath these major posts responsibilities are allocated in a conventional pyramidal way. Problems can, however, arise where an administrative officer's work is primarily carrying out the instructions of a particular committee. One example might be an administrator responsible for the affairs of a large and powerful faculty or school. His loyalty to the dean and the faculty board may well conflict with his responsibilities to his administrative superiors, especially when he is instructed specifically by the dean not to communicate a certain matter to his superiors.

Two points must strike the observer in examining the organization structure of a university. First, the division of work is not based upon the hierarchical relationship normally found in large organizations. Not only is much of the work functionally divided between Council and Senate, despite the former's technically superior position, but it is to a large extent devolved from one committee to another, rather than from one individual to another. Secondly, there is a clear break between the non-hierarchical structure above the level of the department and the existence of hierarchy within departments.

These two aspects, division by function and committee at one level, and division by hierarchy at another, have led to a variety of criticism. Broadly speaking, it may be said that outsiders wish to see an extension of the principle of hierarchy and lay influence, whereas insiders seek a reduction both of hierarchy and lay influence. At the same time, there are those who criticize the division of university affairs into financial and property matters, which on no account must dreamy, impractical academics get their hands on, and purely academic affairs, from which ignorant outsiders must be excluded at all costs.

In one of the most rigorous of the several recent reviews of the constitutions and organization of universities, the Review Body chaired by Mr. Jo Grimond and set up by the Council of Birmingham University, concluded against separation of function between Council and Senate, between finance and academic affairs. In their final report in 1972,[26] the Review Body recommended drastic reform of the existing organization. First, while Court was still to exist with a revised membership, it would cease to be the supreme governing body and would have a consultative and ceremonial function only. Secondly, that the Council would be the supreme governing body of the university in both academic and non-academic matters. Membership of the Council should be revised, however, to include normally 19 'lay' members (including 2 from the Guild of Graduates), 23 academic staff, and 8 students. This new council would be advised on academic matters by a Senate of some 152 members which would mainly consider broad policy issues, and by an academic executive of some 21 members which would be the major decision-making academic body for the day-to-day running of academic affairs.

The draft proposals of the Review Body in an earlier consultative document had been even more radical. The new Council would have worked through two new executives, an academic executive of some 16 members and a finance and general purposes executive of some 20 lay and academic members. Senate in its present form would have disappeared and advice to the Council would have been tendered by a large academic body some 400 strong.

This was rather strong meat for some, especially the existing senators. Some worthwhile arguments were put forward in opposition to the unicameral proposals. Apart from the observation that the traditional system had worked well, and that Senate had *de facto* control of academic matters, the Birmingham Senate argued that its large size had led to the involvement of more persons in decision-making and that it had increasingly had to delegate powers to the faculties and to departments. Unicameral government would reverse these desirable trends. Paradoxically, they also opposed the idea of an academic assembly, believing that it would lack authority.

Thus virtues are made of necessities. The argument of our previous chapter was largely that effectiveness of any kind was sometimes impossible to discern in universities because of the difficulty at present of finding any criteria other than loudness of assertion for judging it. We would add that, in an era when the availability of resources is limited, some effective means of judging and co-ordinating a university's activities would appear to be essential. This simply cannot happen within most universities, when decision-making is in the hands of large bodies whereon is represented every vested interest in the university. The argument for delegation is an appealing one, but it can be carried out by means other than default. Under existing arrangements, it is only by ensuring that the 'real' decisions are taken before the formal meetings that anything can be achieved at all. Far from being critical of those vice-chancellors who have this kind of facility, one should admire their political skill and diligence which allows the existing system to function. As it is, all important Senate decisions are taken in committee. The total body has usually the power only of rejecting a proposal and telling the committee to go back and do its homework again. There may be a case for creating a small standing executive committee, composed of the deans of faculties, to take most of the effective decisions, rather than the alternative of mysterious 'working parties' appearing from no-where. Those, however, who are concerned about the powers of vice-chancellors and of favoured professors, have little alternative but to seek a small decision-making unit with membership based upon election of one kind or another.

The Birmingham Review Body, as well as recommending a change in the relationship between Senate and Council, also suggested reforms at department level. In particular, they stressed their desire to see an ending of the link between the status of the professorial chair and executive headship of a department for life. They advocated both a time limit to any headship and/or an element of rotation within the department for the post. The Birmingham Review Body did, however, suggest that the 'electoral boards' which appointed to chairs should decide the initial period of executive responsibility, which in some cases could be life. Since the Birmingham report, a more radical view of the necessity of ending the notion that the rank of professor must carry executive responsibility has emerged from the Association of University Teachers.[27] The Association's view is that 'professors' should be a title of status, and that chairmen of departments should be selected for short periods, say three years, by the members of the department.

Despite, however, the strong pressures from within universities to 'democratize' university government, there persists a view that what universities need is not less hierarchy, but more. The most famous, or perhaps the most notorious, expression of this 'plain man's view' of universities was the report prepared by the industrial consultants, John Tyzack and Partners for Warwick University in 1968, parts of which were leaked to the outside world by the students who occupied the university registry in February 1970.

The consultants apparently considered Warwick University then to be "certainly inefficient by normal commercial or industrial standards".[28] Although some of this apparent inefficiency concerned financial and 'hotel-keeping' operations, at one point they remarked that the "committee system of government is in danger of running riot". Although their report contained a number of intelligent comments upon the workings of Warwick's committee structure, which appeared fairly typical of British universities, the consultants betrayed a certain amount of (perhaps understandable) impatience with the apparent cost of the structure, both in terms of staff time and the amount of administrative resources tied up in servicing it. Instead, however, of making some attempt to understand and reform the structure in democratic terms, they sought to strengthen the administration's executive powers, under the direct command of the Vice-Chancellor, to the extent of recommending a post of a Deputy Vice-Chancellor, without the security of tenure normal at such a level, and responsible only to the Vice-Chancellor. They used the analogy of a board of directors appointing a general manager. What the Tyzack consultants failed to understand is the difference between the concepts of efficiency and effectiveness. The consultants would presumably have approved a hierarchical structure where information flowed along chosen channels, where co-ordination was simply achieved by a hierarchical relationship and where everyone followed his superior's instructions. Such an organization could not, and never could be, a university in the sense in which that word has been hitherto understood in the English language.

There is no known case in the history of organizations where bureaucratically organized institutions, for that is what Tyzack, and those others who urge universities to be more 'businesslike' imply, have been successful in discovering new knowledge. Nor, in education, have such institutions been known to instil a sense of responsible critical enquiry in their charges. Either they produce technicians, which is entirely appropriate in some cases, or nihilists.

CHAPTER 4

Organization and Performance

It is rather a mystery that some of those who seek to improve the performance of universities should favour an administrative structure which informed opinion no longer considers appropriate in many sectors of industry and commerce. Much of the impetus towards more 'rational' systems of university administration implies that there exists a body of 'sound administrative principles' formed in the world of industry, where the discipline of the market-place ensures that only the best shall survive. Our understanding of the administrative process in industrial firms has, however, advanced a long way indeed from the simplistic 'one best way' propositions that were once held to be universally applicable. Recent research has indicated that there can be no 'universal' management principles applied to industrial firms. This can be illustrated by referring to the conclusion of two celebrated research projects in industrial management.

A comprehensive study[29] of 100 firms with more than 100 employees in one geographical area of Britain, South East Essex, indicated that there was no correlation between successful performance and the use of traditional 'sound organizational principles'. It was found, however, that firms with the same broadly defined production technology shared broadly similar organizational characteristics and that the more successful firms in each category followed a common pattern, in tending to be clustered around the median for each characteristic. Thus, meaningful generalizations may be made of firms with common technological characteristics, but not across these technological divisions, e.g. between one mass-production firm and another, but not between a mass-production firm and a 'process' firm such as an oil refinery. The other study[30] was concerned primarily with firms' abilities to cope with change and innovation. It demonstrated that when prescribing an organizational structure for firms one has to take account of the nature of the markets being served and the pace of technological obsolescence in the industry. Where markets were stable and technological progress slow, as in rayon production, one form of organization, a rigid *mechanistic* form, seemed appropriate. Where existing knowledge was continually being superseded and markets changed rapidly, as in the electronics industry, a form of organization which stressed flexibility and adaptation was appropriate. This latter form, dubbed *organic* by the researchers, was, in effect, an inversion of the *mechanistic* form suitable for routine operations.

Research has indicated other factors which affect the structures of firms. In addition to the effects of technology and of environment outlined above, we have also to take account of the values, norms and aspirations of the work force. This is of importance in understanding the different responses in different industries. For instance, working groups who have traditionally lived closely together and who value social ties, such as miners and dockers, will often respond differently to a particular form of organization structure from, say, workers in car factories who value high earnings above all else. Similarly, it is not unreasonable to suppose that university academic staff, with their long training and high level of education, will not necessarily respond to a structure of organization which may have been found successful in organizing routine clerical workers.

The task to be performed also has to be taken into account. This is closely related to the technology employed. A research project in 'the production of light ions in the thermal neutron fission of uranium 235' is somewhat different from digging a hole in a road, and one would hardly expect these activities to be organized in similar ways. In discussing the structure of universities, it would, therefore, seem wise to pay attention to the goals of the university, to the environment which affects it, especially in the sense of the 'market' the university serves, to the technology used in the university, and to the characteristics, in the broadest sense, of the members of the university. Only after considering factors such as these can one dare to suggest appropriate structures of organization of universities.

About goals we do not need to add much to our previous discussion. We should note the general consensus that overall university goals can be considered in three main categories: research, teaching, and social. The explicit mention of a social goal is to highlight the broad educative effect which attendance at university is claimed to have in addition to the simple acquisition of knowledge and understanding of a field of study, which is what may be meant by a 'teaching' goal. The purpose of differentiating is that it is not self-evident that any particular form of organization is appropriate to all three. At least one commentator has suggested that the organizational needs of a research system and of a teaching system are markedly different.[31]

We may approach each of these goals in turn. To begin with research: how does a university see its research effort contributing to the greater benefit of society? Opinion can vary among different universities. Some see research being applied to the solution of existing problems. More usually, however, research is seen by academic staff as being concerned with fundamental problems which often have no immediate application. Clearly, emphasis will vary according to subject group as well as according to university. We would expect most engineers to have a more 'practical' orientation than pure scientists, social scientists to be more concerned with immediate problems than arts men. There is little doubt, however, that in most universities the pecking order favours the more abstract against the 'useful' subjects.

In the nation's scientific research effort, it is recognized that 'pure' research as an end in itself takes place only within the universities. The other main university contribution to scientific research is 'basic' research which may be defined as open-ended in scope, but within a certain predetermined area of concern. Some large firms and government research centres also contribute to this field. In industry, most research is 'applied' in nature, i.e. trying to convert ideas discovered in basic or pure research into more precise products, and 'developmental' which is the engineering of the research project into a prototype article.

In 'pure' and basic research, it has been historically accepted that direction of the researcher was impossible. The individual had to make his own research decisions. One Nobel prize-winner has been quoted as saying of some of his former students who were now colleagues, "I've left them to make their own decisions. I don't think there should be such a thing as a director of research, even at graduate student level."[32] Another claimed he did not propose experiments for others to do; he simply criticized their experimental designs and helped others interpret their results. The image of the 'lone inventor' is a strong one.

Recent investigation, however, has indicated that the best performance achieved in science is not when researchers are left on their own to get on with the job. Nor have researchers had great success when subjected to traditional kinds of managerial directions. The most comprehensive study[33] yet conducted into the organization of scientific laboratories demonstrated that performance was highest when many others apart from the researcher were involved in deciding his technical assignment and when both the scientist and his immediate superior, or the scientist and his colleagues, had considerable influence upon managerial decisions. Earlier studies upon the behaviour of research directors indicated that a greater sense of purpose and motivation was found in laboratories where the directors had a *participative* style of leadership, as compared with laboratories with *directive* or *laissez-faire* inclined leaders. In the participative laboratories, most decisions were taken jointly after discussion between superior and subordinate, subordinates felt they had some influence on their directors, contact was frequent and they had little sense of being on their own.[34]

These results seem to indicate that in the organization of research work, excessive individualism is likely to be counterproductive, and directive authoritarian approaches have little effect. A middle way has to be found which stresses open communication and participative decision-making.

The organizational design required, not surprisingly, does not appear to differ greatly from that found in firms in highly innovative industries which employ large numbers of highly qualified manpower. The study by Burns and Stalker was probably the first to point to the need for different organizational principles to be used in the management of such firms. Their ideas have since been greatly refined and applied by some American companies, operating in 'high technology'. Particularly, one may point to the Californian firm of T.R.W. Systems Inc., very prominent in the development of the Apollo programme, of whose 12,500 employees in 1967, over 4,000 were professional engineers and about half of these held advanced degrees.[35] In this firm, organization was not at all on traditional hierarchical lines. Seniority of status was recognized, but not bureaucratic authority. Much 'management' was on project-group lines, with great emphasis on face-to-face communication and levelling of status distinctions. Emphasis was placed on 'interpersonal competence', in plain language, getting along with others, and inability to do this ultimately meant dismissal.

This open style is not the consequence of managers reading books upon good human relations, but is demanded by the tasks which have to be fulfilled. Universities perhaps do not have to fulfil the kinds of schedules T.R.W. had, and thus they can afford to be more 'soft-centred' in their treatment of non-conformists. The industrial experience does, however, point in a vivid way to the kind of organizational form one can expect when scientific or technological innovation is sought. Whatever the detail of the design, the most successful organization of research is open, collaborative and hierarchical only in the sense that knowledge and expertise are respected.

In the organization of teaching, however, it may be argued that this is hardly an innovative situation. Teaching in universities is the passing on of what is known already. The problem is simply one of organizing this transmission process in an orderly and economic fashion. In other words, the teaching function of universities is susceptible to a high degree of bureaucratization. A first-year class in mathematics in 1973 presents the same kinds of problems as a similar class in 1972 or in 1962. Thus procedures can be routinized, rules formulated to make sure that students and lecturers do meet in the same rooms at the same time and that the simple technology of required chalk and blackboard, or of overhead projector, are available for use. It may, then, be argued that the complex system of government demanded by universities in Britain is hardly appropriate to their main duty of instructing their under-graduates. A more routinized, hierarchical model would be both efficient and more effective in terms of the teaching function.

This argument, however, can only refer to the manner in which teaching is carried out. It cannot refer to what is taught. E. Allison Peers, writing as 'Bruce Truscot', in his classic *Redbrick University,* referred to the pre-war student who could turn up at his provincial university with the lecture notes his father had taken a generation before and notice that the same lecturer had hardly varied a word in the intervening years. This is not a pattern of higher education which commands wide-spread support today. It has, however, been suggested that one of the main reasons why the new universities created since 1961 were able to recruit high quality staff was that many of the brightest teachers in the established civic universities despaired of breaking the frustrating fetters which often bound the curricula and teaching methods. In many of the established universities and departments, routinization was carried to a high degree and innovation was hardly conspicuous. Organization was basically hierarchical, few senates had any but token representation of non-professorial staff, and government was effectively in the control of a professorial oligarchy.

It is striking to compare this traditional model with what happened in many of the new universities, where not only new departments were being established, but new kinds of courses were being devised. Many of these involved high degrees of collaboration and non-hierarchical decision-making, both with-in departments and across departments. Some staff who taught the 'first runs' of many of these new courses in the sixties will now confess privately to the impression they had of total 'shambles' in the early years. This refers not to the building-site environment of the early years, but to the administrative and teaching arrangements. Co-ordination was achieved not by committee work or by circulating memos, but by the enthusiasm and commitment of the staff. As, however, the rate of growth tapered off, and as courses became more established, a process of routinization set in, which corroded or even destroyed the spirit of the early years.

Probably the best example of the importance of organic-style organization of teaching has been in the Open University. In presenting a new course there, a team basis of organization is essential. Some six to nine people working full-time, plus several others part-time, have to co-ordinate their work on a kind of free-flow basis. There can be no question of one lecturer being responsible for teaching a complete course, as frequently happens in conventional universities. The necessity for all the support material to be produced according to a strict schedule makes it imperative that everyone lives in each other's pocket. Not only do the teachers have to keep in close touch with each other, but BBC producers, educational technologists, editors, and research assistants, have to be fully-fledged members of course teams. In some faculties, indeed, there are effectively no departments as such, simply a collection of course teams. It will be interesting to observe whether the educational aspects of the Open University will become subject to a process of bureaucratization as courses become established and the presentation of a completed course becomes a matter of routine. On the other hand, it is possible that other factors which affect the teaching function at the Open University will force a continuation of the more organic approach.

For the organization of academic work is not governed only by the purpose of the university. The environment, the teaching technology, the nature of the student, affect the organization of teaching in all universities, but they are particularly highlighted in the Open University. The environment is possibly the most important of these factors. In most universities, the external examiner for each department or course is usually the only person from outside the university who scrutinizes the teaching work of a department, and in many this is done only cursorily. The work of the Open University, however, is available to anyone who cares to switch on his radio or television at the appropriate time and who cares to purchase the set books which are freely available at academic booksellers. Moreover, the whole concept of the Open University was not altogether popular in some sections of academic and political opinion, and staff who had accepted posts at the Open University knew that they had to be on their mettle.

The nature of the technology employed in the teaching process also affected organization. There was the importance of deadlines, if home equipment was to be specified, purchased and supplied to students. There were printing deadlines and broad-casting schedules to be met, too. The relative novelty of broadcasting, and to some extent the other methods of instruc-tion, meant that the academic staff had to rely to a great extent upon the expertise and skills of educational technologists, BBC producers, and the like. Thus the technology used meant that expertise had to be shared and authority diffused. The fact that many students had little recent experience of a formal educational process, together with the fact that they were scattered throughout the length and breadth of the land, often far from suitable library facilities, meant that they could not be left to forage for themselves, as often happens in traditional universities. (Indeed, many staff argue that the foraging process is an essential part of the 'teaching to learn for themselves' aspect of higher education.) For these reasons reading material had to be detailed and supplied to each student. In other words, the amount of preparation for the course had to be far more thorough than is ordinarily the case.

For all of these reasons, the successful organization of Open University courses had to have this organic flavour. In the new universities and in the Open University, for a time, teaching was the dominant concern of academic staff. For once, per-formance as an academic was measured in terms of teaching ability. For several years, teaching was the prime activity of the institution. In the new universities, the imperative was the presence of students who had to be taught, at the Open University the demands of a new technology and the eyes of the world were additional motivators. In the newer universities, innovation has often given way to routine; in the Open University, public exposure may mean that teaching will always have to be updated and of high quality. Thus the bureaucratic hand will have to lie on it lightly.

A third task of the university as part of its educative function, in addition to straightforward instruction in skills, is that of somehow 'improving' its students into being better citizens as well as being better technicians. Broadly, this is the concept that the Robbins Committee tried to define under its goal headings of a generalized, not over-specialized instruction and of the transmission of a common culture. As so often happens in social science, it is easier to give examples than to give an adequate definition. If the university succeeds in this task, its graduating student will feel a pride and a loyalty to his Alma Mater which will last until the end of his days. This will not be a matter of simple nostalgia for memories of youth, but will involve also a sense of values which one associates with Glasgow-men or Cambridge-men. In its more trivial manifestation this quality is exemplified by the wearing of respective college and university scarves by Oxford and Cambridge graduates at the annual boat race or rugby match between their successors. At a more serious level, many American universities frequently rely upon this sense of lifelong membership when they seek to raise funds. Indeed, the *alumni*, the American term for their graduates, can represent a considerable source of finance, and sometimes power, on the American campus.

The elusiveness of this idea, that education at a university is more than simply a matter of learning and understanding a set syllabus, is partly caused by the fact that its importance varies widely between different universities and even between different faculties. It is clear that this inculcation of value, or socialization function of a university is understood and implemented at some institutions, pre-eminently Oxbridge colleges, and is, in effect, completely ignored at some others, which perhaps had better remain unnamed. We are not concerned here to try to define the concept closely, but rather to identify the means whereby it is implemented. One difficulty is that although we recognize a 'socialization' function in almost all universities, the goals of this process appear to vary. For instance, whilst Oxbridge has been criticized for its 'finishing school mentality' and for overconcern with gracious living, a technological university, whose academic instruction is 'sandwiched' between work in industry, is arguably overconcerned with the 'relevance' of what it does, and with attempting to ensure that its students do not lose sight of mundane matters. If we agree that some such 'social' task exists, and even the self-styled 'revolutionaries' who complain of the processing of students into products acceptable to the nasty capitalist system seem to agree that it does, how can it best be implemented? Or, to emphasize our current concern, how can it be organized?

Little systematic research has been carried out in this area.

All that we can do is to identify the methods and organization used where the socialization goal seems to be important. The form of organization in itself does not appear to matter especially. Clearly, the ancient collegiate universities place great importance on this activity, and appear to have gained considerable success in carrying it out. But so also do some of the non-collegiate institutions. One of our major problems is identifying the ingredients of 'success'.

Two common factors which appear to be important are smallness of scale and residence in or near the university. By and large, the smaller the basic unit, and the higher the proportion of students which live within easy walking distance of the campus, the greater the chance of success for a socialization function. Other factors which appear to matter are the proportion of free time students have available to devote to non-instructional activities, the ability to join and take part in societies and clubs, and the amount of time and interest staff are prepared to give to instruction and to non-formal interaction with students.

It does appear that the form of organization is less important than the methods used ('technology') to achieve this 'social' aim. We suggest that a strong case exists for more attention being paid to the technology employed by the university to achieve a 'social' goal which aims to increase the students' potential as a human being as well as his potential as a technical specialist. We may note that this 'technology' exists even when the university appears to renounce any formal activity in this area. Thus, for instance, in the matter of how to organize students in residence, while English universities might debate the merits of residential colleges as against halls of residence, or against university-approved lodgings, in Scotland the official attitude until recently was that how students spent their extra-curricular time was no concern of the university authorities. One might argue that the traditional Scottish approach, which treated students as adults, was the one most likely to teach self-reliance and independence of judgement in their charges.

As far as organization is concerned, apart from trying to base organization on units of small size, the most important factor appears to be to decentralize. The lesson for academic organization of the history of Oxbridge colleges is not the sherry-

E

sipping cameraderie of yester-year, but the importance of frequent face-to-face instruction. Just as any survey of how universities succeed in the socializing function will probably point to the value of the small unit, any look at the teaching process from that viewpoint is likely to conclude that the decentralized course is likely to be best in furthering any 'social' function: the ideal being the antithesis of the mass-lecture to which simple-minded economists are likely to be leading us.

Overall, then, when we view the organization of the university, we have to consider how any structure relates to the objectives the university strives to attain. Further, any structure suited to the objectives of the university is constrained by the technology available to it, and by the characteristics of those being organized, a subject we look at in detail later. We have indicated, however, that university teaching staff place great value on individual freedom in research and teaching methods and in being governed by a representative system rather than by appointed officials. Because there is a fairly wide element of choice over the methods to be employed in approaching objectives, there can be substantial difference in detail between the formal structures of organization of universities. Nevertheless, the elements of substantial autonomy of individuals, together with a representative system, somehow must be present. Moreover, it is vital to remember that the structure of organization is only an outline of how things can work. Another essential factor in the successful organization of a university is an understanding of the groups which comprise it. They are not passive instruments of the structure, but, by a process of interacting both through and outwith the formal channels, they determine what is the real system of government.

CHAPTER 5

Membership Characteristics

'Organizations are simply the sums of their parts' might be the motif of this chapter. In discussing the goals and organization structures of universities, there is a temptation to attribute to these abstractions a life and will of their own. The importance of ongoing goals and organization structures in shaping people's behaviour should not be minimized. It is well, however, to reflect that decisions are made and policies planned and implemented by individuals and groups of individuals. Whilst the behaviour of members of a university is 'constrained' by the roles they play in it, by the authority system, by the goals of the institution, their behaviour is also affected by the values which they have come to hold as citizens and as individuals and by their perception of the environment with which the university has to deal.

A professor will be constrained by the way others will expect him to behave within the university, by the administrative demands of his job, by the decisions which are referred to him, by his own place in the university's system of government, by his perception of the goals of the university from his own particular department, and by other influences which arise within the university. To his work at university he will bring not only an understanding and at least minimal loyalty to the institution, but he will also bring personal aspirations and values and a style of behaviour governed partly by extra-organizational influences. His attitudes and actions are dictated not merely by memos from the vice-chancellor's office or by the turbulence of his department's relations with another, but also by his own level of ambition, and his own interests. His demeanour is a reflection not merely of his relationships with his colleagues and subordinates, but also of those with his wife and children. His behaviour is a reflection not only of that expected of a professor, but also of that expected of a human being.

Therefore, before we attempt to understand behaviour within a university, we ought to understand something of the groups which constitute it. Obviously, we cannot be concerned with the minutiae outlined above, but, equally obviously, we cannot ignore the values and aspirations held by the different groups who together comprise the university.

There is a sense, also, in which the university, more than most organizations, is simply the people who comprise it. Take the managers, technicians, and workers away from a factory wherein they manufacture aircraft and you cannot call them an aircraft manufacturing firm. Take away the building and equipment from the students and staff and, arguably, you still have a university. The university is the teachers and the students, nothing else. We have already pointed out that the medieval latin word *universitas* meant simply 'community'.

Today this concept of the university still has relevance, in the sense that mention is always made in charters and elsewhere of the 'members' of the university, in effect, the academic staff and students. All other personnel, except some specific exceptions, usually the Registrar and the Librarian, are employees. This category includes all other administrative staff from highly qualified architects and accountants to car park attendants. More importantly, we have witnessed in the past decade several 'migrations' which emphasize that a university is essentially a society of its members. Several of the former Colleges of Advanced Technology with no university tradition moved their locations upon being upgraded. The most striking example was the move of the Bristol C.A.T. some 12 miles to Bath. Admittedly, no established university could move its location without the acquiescence of the University Grants Committee. Nevertheless, when an urban vice-chancellor whose expansion plans are being thwarted by civic authorities publicly muses about the attractions of a green field site elsewhere, his opponents have to recognize that such moves are not without precedent, even in modern times.

Any discussion of the composition of the university, therefore, must begin with the two groups of university members. In addition to the members, any discussion of modern university has to take account of the administrative staff. In examining 'administrative staff' we may find it convenient to discuss only 'management level' administrators. Most university technical and ancillary staff are increasingly organized by trade unions, who further their members' interests exactly as they would in any industrial establishment.

In examining these groups we cannot pretend that our account of each of them is comprehensive. Our own interest is mainly to highlight the features that affect the government of the university and the organization and administration of its activities.

Academic Staff

First, we must look at the academic staff of the modern British university. Numbers of full-time academic staff paid wholly from university funds rose by 45 per cent from 9,869 in 1951 to 14,276 in 1961, and then doubled to 27,974 in the nine years to 1970. In addition, a further 5,291 staff paid for wholly or partly by external sources should be added to this last figure.

The numbers of staff at each institution parallels its student population, although there are proportionately more technologists per student than average and proportionately fewer social scientists. Numbers may vary from institution to institution, but grades of staff and the salary scales do not. The common salary structure is a fairly recent post-war phenomenon.

The grades of staff are threefold: professor, reader or senior lecturer, and lecturer. In 1970, 12 per cent of all staff (3,354) were professors. Most professors are heads of department, but frequently in large departments several professors may rotate the headship, and there are also personal, titular or research professors who have few formal powers but who have the rank, salary range and perquisites of full professors.

Readers and senior lecturers are now paid on the same scale. In 1970 this grade accounted for 19.7 per cent of all staff (5,522) paid wholly from university funds. Traditionally, readers have ranked higher and are usually, though by no means always, appointed for their personal distinction in research. Senior lectureships are often associated with teaching ability and frequently these are filled by internal promotion. Readerships still tend to carry higher status, as if they were more a sub-professorial rank, rather than simply a senior form of lectureship.

The lecturer grade is the career grade, and by far the largest, comprising 64.8 per cent (18,133) of all staff in 1970. The two important qualifications to make are, first, that upon appointment a lecturer is on probation for three years (exceptionally four years) before his appointment is confirmed, and secondly, that he has to pass an 'efficiency bar' after five years post-probationary service, i.e. usually when passing from the eighth or ninth point on the seventeen-point salary scale. His performance is at that time considered by some kind of review body with some representatives from outside his own department. Attitudes to this bar vary from university to university. Some universities have looked upon the bar as being tantamount to a two-part salary scale and insist upon a case being made for a lecturer passing it. Needless to say, the teachers' professional body, the Association of University Teachers, has actively fought this approach, and many universities tend to agree with the association that passing the bar should be automatic, except when it can be shown explicitly that a lecturer's performance has been less than satisfactory.

Since 1972, the number of senior staff, i.e. professors, readers and senior lecturers, should not exceed 40 per cent of the total academic staff in any one university. Although there are variations between universities, the existence of this overall limit restricts the efforts of any one university from trying to attract staff to any particular area of study, except at the expense of another. Such limits also restrict the universities' ability to recruit staff of high calibre in those subjects such as engineering or some management sciences where earnings can be high in industry and commerce, for those possessing the required skills.

We may notice that, whilst in the early twenties the professors made up nearly a third of all university staff, today they represent just over one tenth of the total. Whilst the financial differentiation between lecturer and professor has greatly narrowed over the years, the lower proportion of professors has meant increased power and status for the professoriate. In considering recent reforms of university constitutions we should bear in mind that the automatic representation given to professors in the Senates was originally a right accorded to about one third, or more, of the teaching staff.

In all of the above, however, we must make exceptions of the universities of Oxford and Cambridge. The proportion of professors there is much smaller than elsewhere and unlike other universities they are always in a minority on university governing bodies. In some cases they may even be paid less than some non-professors! The reason for this lies in the rather complex way emoluments are earned, partly from the university and partly from the colleges. In brief, what it amounts to is that the 'average' lecturer-fellow is paid something like 15–20 per cent more than his counterpart elsewhere. It has been argued in justification that Oxbridge staff work longer hours than their counterparts in other universities, although it is not, we think, commonly held that working conditions at England's two ancient universities are particularly unpleasant or more arduous than at any other institution. A salary differential in favour of those universities with the highest social status and the best library facilities is hardly likely to 'level up' the others.

Traditionally, however, the academic teaching profession as a whole has been characterized by high social prestige, combined, as has not been uncommon in Great Britain, with relatively low earnings. It has been an élite profession in two senses. Firstly, in the obvious one of being the intellectual mentors of a society becoming increasingly education-conscious. Its élite status was emphasized by its smallness. In 1938 the total number of university teachers in Great Britain was less than 4,500. Secondly, it gained social status from the way in which attendance at England's ancient universities became almost obligatory for the governing classes of the country. This social esteem, however, was not reflected in the remuneration it gave. Throughout the inter-war period, no less a body than the University Grants Committee continually chided the universities to improve the financial position of their staffs.

Today, whilst the financial position of the university teacher compares better with that of other groups in the education world, pleas from the professional association-cum-trade union, the Association of University Teachers, for automatic comparison with posts in the higher civil service and in industry, fall upon deaf ears in Whitehall. Even in 1963, when the Association's pay claim was referred to the National Incomes Commission, a statutory body which became highly unpopular for its efforts to restrain wage and salary rises, the Commission declared that university teachers were up to 20 per cent underpaid.

The origins of the low salary tradition lies in the historical role of Oxford and Cambridge universities as religious seminaries run by celibate priests. Until 1878, it was necessary for a teaching fellow of an Oxford college to be an ordained priest of the Church of England and not until the same year were the now apparently godless fellows allowed the distraction of the sacrament of matrimony. Within the colleges, however, the standard of living was high and fellows had little need of substantial stipends. At the same time, the colleges and universities founded in nineteenth century England made substantial provision for the professors, who were, apart from temporary assistants, the teaching staff. The problem, in the pre-1914 and inter-war years, was that the neglected temporary assistants became permanent, and expanded into being the profession's effective career grade.

Paradoxically, the recent comparative improvement in the financial lot of university teaching staff coincides with a probable diminution of their still considerable social prestige. To some extent this may only reflect the reduced exclusiveness of a profession of over 30,000 compared with one of less than 5,000. However, it may also reflect the fact that the university teacher of today is likely to have a different social and educational background from his counterpart of past years. In other words, he is less likely to be a product of a private school and of Oxbridge.

To talk of the 'typical' academic is virtually impossible. Taking highest common factors, however, whereas it might have been true between the wars that the 'typical' academic might have been an Oxbridge arts graduate from a private or direct-grant school, today the most typical would be a science graduate from a large civic university and a grammar school. The Oxbridge domination has diminished only gradually. In numerical terms, their influence declines yearly. Their social prestige will, however, remain so long as some 50 per cent of their annual undergraduate intake is drawn from private schools and while their intake of children of manual workers remains at around 10 per cent, as opposed to figures of around 40 per cent at some of the larger civic and Scottish universities.

As we have observed, the association between England's ancient universities and the governing élites is one of the bases of the high social prestige of the university teachers. In the past, the numerical, as well as social dominance of Oxbridge, has meant that many university teachers in Britain share an educational experience and sense of academic values with those who wield commercial and especially governmental power in the country. Despite the difficulties the A.U.T. has had in salary negotiations—perhaps it is significant that the A.U.T. has relatively few members in England's ancient universities—university spokesmen could usually find sympathetic ears in Westminster or Whitehall. The universities could not have asked for more sterling defenders of university independence than successive Treasury civil servants countering the demands of the post-1945 Public Accounts Committee of the House of Commons that greater financial control over university finances should be exercised by the legislature. We may witness the alacrity with which the government of the day disowned the Prices and Incomes Board's suggestion in 1968 that students might have something to contribute to an assessment of the teaching ability of their lecturers.

In terms of university government, the Oxbridge influence has been important in spreading notions of academic democracy, and in countering any incipient cult of the professoriate which might have infiltrated from the Continent. It is difficult to underestimate the importance of the Oxbridge connection in terms of teachers' orientations to academic organization. Even in 1962 almost one-third of all non-medical university teachers in England and Wales and Northern Ireland were graduates of Oxford and Cambridge Universities, as were 55 per cent of Arts professors and 49 per cent of Science professors, and 23 of the 27 Vice-Chancellors. Thus, it seems fair to assume that something of the Oxbridge approaches to academic government has a fairly firm base in British universities.

As to other values which affect the general orientation of the British academic, 'hard' information is not easy to come by or to interpret. One approach, following that of Chapter 2, might be to inquire what goal the academic has. Within each university, what is he trying to achieve and why? What is he getting out of it? It is unlikely to be money. Although, for some groups, arts, divinity, and some social scientists, there are no directly comparable non-teaching occupations which pay substantially better, for the great bulk of university teachers of science, engineering, business subjects, law, architecture, and others, greater financial rewards can usually be gained in industry, commerce or public services. Even for the arts subjects, it can be argued that, as young men or women, present university teachers could well have opted for a management or civil service career.

In discussing financial rewards, we must make passing reference to a new stereotype of the university world, that of the academic entrepreneur. It must be noted that these words are used in two different senses. In this country, usually the term refers to those who use their university post as a secure base from which to run what amounts to a private consultancy business, or as a postal address from which to travel to all corners of the globe on academic or quasi-academic affairs. Although, when carried to excess, these private activities must be condemned, there does still exist a real problem. Not only are greater financial rewards to be found outside the university in many subject areas, but it is certainly arguable that for an engineer, architect, management scientist, and many others, 'keeping up with their subject' entails continuing contact with latest practice and development, which can only be obtained by participating in it. Most universities have now come to terms with this problem, either by placing clear limits on how much time may be devoted to external activities or by getting staff to work through a university-owned and directed consultancy company, which not only keeps some control on activities, but also allows the university to recover some of its overhead costs.

The term can also be used, however, in another sense. In the United States, for instance, it usually refers to the professional fund-raising academic who elicits grants from industry and federal government to set up substantial research centres upon a campus, officially under the aegis of the university, but in practice being virtually independent of it. Given the academic pecking order, good staff are attracted to full-time research work, or to appointments half in the research centre or institute and half in a university department. Usually, the university's teaching effort declines in quality and the university exercises less and less control over the activities carried out in its name by the research directors. Undoubtedly, both forms of entrepreneur exist on British campuses, but on most, such activities have hitherto been confined to a small minority. Given that universities do exercise some effective control over staffs' external activities, whether or not these activities expand depends upon how each university sees its purpose, and to what extent its environment allows it to pursue that purpose.

It is part of our overall argument that a prevailing characteristic of universities today is their diversity. Part of the reason for this diversity is a growth of specialization. The teacher of today will be more specialized than ten years ago and certainly than twenty years ago. His department will be larger and more self-contained. His relations with other departments and with the central administration will be more formalized than previously. A consequence of this process of specialization and formalization is often the growth of what can be called professionalization. Instead of being a lecturer at X University who teaches economics, he will become an industrial economist in the economics department of X University. In other words, he identifies with the discipline and not with the university.

This is a phenomenon well documented in social science. Usually the concept of a 'professional' orientation has been developed in order to highlight the different values and assumptions about organization held by highly-educated practising specialists, from the administrative concepts and orientations traditionally held by managers and administrators. The administrator sees the organization as being made up of men with limited skills who have to be controlled and co-ordinated, through an administrative hierarchy. The 'professional', on the other hand, sees the organization as being peopled by qualified people who can use their skills to solve any technical problem. They are controlled, not by a hierarchy, but by a sense of values which all of them share, and which have been inculcated in them during their long academic and professional training.

It is possible, therefore, to identify, especially in Britain, a profession of university teaching to which this concept of professionalization can be applied. One may argue that professors do not need to be controlled by any higher rank because they all broadly share the same values and assumptions and thus, left to themselves, will conduct their departments' activities in a broadly similar way. Such co-ordination as is needed can be implemented through committee meetings or through the office of the vice-chancellor, so rare is there a need for his intervention. The concept, however, can be looked at in a different way. The profession will not be that of university teaching, but that of the discipline he teaches. He is not a professional university teacher, he is a professional mechanical engineer, lawyer, organic chemist, and so on. In such a case, when a specialist identifies himself more as a practitioner of a discipline and less as a member of a particular institution, there is a twofold effect. On the one hand, he will lose interest in the affairs of his institution and leave much administrative activity to those who have a taste for such work, be they autocratic professors, professional administrators, or more radical 'activist' colleagues. On the other hand, in identifying more with a profession, he will reject hierarchical values and the relevance or legitimacy of instructions from non-professionals.

The professionally-oriented academic will seek rewards not necessarily within his own university, but in winning the respect of his colleagues in the profession at large. He seeks advancement either in promotion or in transferring to a more prestigious department or centre. It goes without saying that he is research-oriented rather than teaching-oriented. He is not primarily interested in being promoted within the university he happens to work in, as a reward for having made himself a valued member of that community, through either teaching or more general duties, such as representing his colleagues in the university's committee structure. Together with seeking acclaim from his fellow-practitioners, the true 'professional' recognizes as his only control, apart from an ethical code, the collective disapprobation of his equals. This aspect of 'professional' control is best exemplified in the control of law and medicine by the Law Societies and by the General Medical Council respectively. Economists and engineers may not have developed their professional power to this degree of organization, but there is little doubt that they share the general sentiments of lawyers and medical men towards this kind of body.

The lesson of this analysis for universities is not that 'professionals' will accept any kind of administrative arrangement, provided that they have sufficient autonomy to follow their own careers—but that universities must make a conscious attempt to flatten the administrative hierarchy and to ensure that control mechanisms are in the hands of a body which can be truly said to represent all the academic staff. We may sum up the difference between the conventional management approach and the basis of professional organization by saying that university teachers must not be judged in administrative terms by their superiors, but in professional terms by their seniors.

This overall picture is borne out by the best attempt yet to find some quantitative basis for these known trends. A. H. Halsey and Martin Trow followed up the sample survey made by Claus Moser for the Robbins Committee on Higher Education, by sending to the Robbins respondents an additional questionnaire designed to probe attitudes and values. In part, their survey[36] fills out the 'social arithmetic' of the changing composition of the profession brought out by the Robbins survey. Two cautionary points should, however, be noted. One is that the survey was carried out in 1965, just before the biggest expansion took place, an expansion of staff as well as of students, and what was typical in 1965 will not necessarily be typical in 1975. Secondly, much of the 'social portrait' information is inconclusive and Halsey and Trow's conclusions are frequently conjectural. In terms of our preoccupation with organization, it is perhaps significant that 37–38 per cent of teachers at both major and minor redbrick universities would prefer a similar post at another university, compared with 23 and 24 per cent in Scotland and at London respectively, and only 8 per cent at Oxford and Cambridge. By far the most popularly preferred destination was, of course, Oxford or Cambridge, although it is not clear whether this was for reasons of social prestige, academic prestige, better working conditions and facilities, better living environment or more pay.

One aspect of their study which has a bearing upon our earlier discussion of the 'professionalization' of university staff, as well as with the commonly expressed view from Whitehall, amongst others, that university staff are obsessed with research to the exclusion of teaching, was the response to questions on this subject. Perhaps to the surprise of many, over one-third (36 per cent) claimed to be primarily interested in teaching and only one-tenth claimed to be heavily interested in research. The remaining 54 per cent admitted a leaning towards research, but claimed considerable interest in teaching. In addition, 22 per cent strongly disagreed that research should be their first duty as academics and a further 43 per cent disagreed, with reservations. Substantial differences were, however, found between different faculties. Medicine claimed the strongest commitment to research, followed by natural science, whereas technology and social science showed least interest, although the social scientists had as 'good' a publication record as the arts faculties.

Of relevance to our argument in Chapter 2 about the university's reward structure was the widespread agreement that promotion was too dependent upon publication. This was assented to, with or without reservations, by 76 per cent of the total sample. Although, predictably, this figure included more than 90 per cent of the non-medical staff, it also included between two-thirds and two-fifths of the 'researchers', the largest number of assenting 'researchers' being in the natural sciences. There were, however, considerable differences between the 'teachers' and the 'researchers'. Briefly, the researchers tended more towards the 'professional' model, more towards a 'cosmopolitan' view of universities and career possibilities. Their attitudes towards university organization also varied. They tended to agree more strongly with criticisms of traditional methods of organization and to favour in greater numbers more democratic reforms. Of the total sample, 57 per cent agreed strongly or with reservations that most British university departments would be better run by the method of circulating chairmanship than by a permanent head of department, 77 per cent that "Redbrick universities tended to be dominated all too often by a professorial oligarchy", the same percentage, that departments with more than eight members should have more than one professor, although only 40 per cent thought that a professorship ought to be a normal expectation of an academic career.

Overall, there seems little doubt that British university

teachers are unhappy with the dominant and traditional hierarchical model of organization traditionally found in the non-collegiate universities. It is clear that even in 1965 the British academic was dissatisfied with how universities were organized, and events since then have hardly dispelled this impression. The new policy of the Association of University Teachers to seek to end the principle of the 'one head of department appointed until retirement' is symbolic. The Association, on the whole, tends not to take controversial stances in academic or political matters. It seeks to be active in those fields where there is a large measure of agreement, which is why, historically, it has concentrated almost solely upon improving salaries and conditions.

It is difficult to generalize about academic attitudes. The implication of the Halsey and Trow study is that a large number view teaching as a pleasurable activity. On the other hand, the large urban universities have achieved a historical notoriety for indifference towards students, to which staff have undoubtedly contributed. Nevertheless, we are sure that there is a far greater awareness of and sympathy for the problems of students today than there was ten years ago in the large universities. Even the most traditional of universities will at least be running trial schemes of alternative means of assessing students' performances. Several universities allocate every student a tutor who is required to meet the student at least once every term, to discuss any kind of problem the student may be having. To the inhabitant of a small residential community like Keele, St. Andrews, or an Oxford college, the above may appear appallingly elementary. But from first-hand experience, we can verify that just over ten years ago in a major urban university with over 500 years' experience of dealing with students, none of these measures existed and few were contemplated.

Students

What, then, of the students? The measurement employed for gauging the size of a university is numbers of students. Currently, they number some 295,000, having been some 107,700 in 1960. By 1976/77 there should be some 306,000 students at British universities. These figures understate the overall position of British 18-plus higher education since by

1976/77 there will be another 270,000 students in other streams of advanced further education.

Clearly, over the years, the concept of what it is to be a student has altered. From one being trained to take his place in a cultured and educated ruling élite, a student is now generally being given a high level of technical expertise. The pressmen's word 'technocrat' will apply to the social scientist and the engineer. Traditionalists will mourn that only in the arts faculty does the soul of the university survive. In terms of stereotypes, the popular conception of the 'student' appears to be one who is hairy, unkempt, radical, sexually permissive, privileged and ungrateful. In terms of a profile of the 'average' student, nothing could be more at odds with the truth.

The great majority of students are sober, hard-working, responsible, and more sexually restrained than the majority of their age group. Out of some 460,000 students in Great Britain, it is not difficult to find some to fit the stereotype which has been largely created by the manner in which elements of the Press and television present students to the public. We may take as an example the events at Stirling University on October 12, 1972, when a demonstration by the students (who felt that the university's expenditure on ceremonial events was excessive) was held to be insulting to the monarch. The country was apparently outraged by an older student drinking from a wine bottle as the Queen passed by. The detractors of the Stirling students scarcely paused to consider that the head of state, guarded only by a harassed detective in the background, had strolled smilingly through this supposedly menacing crowd. The Queen's good humour and tolerance were apparently lost upon the leader writers of the popular press, in their determination to sensationalize and trivialize the incident.

Not that popular hostility to students is anything new. In the middle ages, 'town and gown' riots, in which people were killed, were not uncommon. In the English university towns, public hostility to students is allegedly endemic. At the time of the arrests and trial of the Cambridge students accused of breaking up a dinner held by the Greek Tourist Authority, the Press had no difficulty in finding quotations from Cambridge burghers which made those of Mr. Justice Stevenson seem positively benign. One article written at the time was able to allege that Cambridge police 'hated' the students. No doubt an overstatement, but the diligent unearthing of seldom-used laws under which to prosecute the students, by the Chief Constable of Mid-Anglia, hardly indicated indifference or indulgence.

What kind of true profile can we draw? The 'average' student in Britain is middle class, attends a university more than thirty miles from his home, is equally likely to live either in a university college or hall, or independently in a flat or lodgings. In presenting a numerical picture, the figures for 1970–71 show 192,400 undergraduates, plus 42,800 postgraduate students, making 235,200 in all. Of these, 166,000 were men and 68,300 were women. Of the total 39 per cent lived in university colleges or halls, 45 per cent in flats or lodgings and 16 per cent at home.

Within this overall picture, there were wide variations between different universities and between different subject groups. For instance, the proportion of students living at home in large universities varied from two-thirds at Glasgow to less than one per cent at Bristol. The general pattern, however, is for the proportion of home-based students to be below 20 per cent. Apart from Scotland, where Strathclyde (64 per cent), Heriot-Watt (45 per cent) and Aberdeen (30 per cent) have high proportions, only London (23 per cent) and City (25 per cent) and some city-based universities such as Liverpool (20 per cent), Cardiff (18 per cent) and Newcastle (16 per cent) have substantial proportions living at home. Among subjects, the obvious difference is the proportion of women students. High proportions of women students are found in arts, social and business studies and low proportions in technology. Whilst, in general, these proportions simply reflect the degree of attraction of these subjects to women, and the social conditioning which occurs in many schools, effectively dissuading girls from studying physical sciences, it is known that some faculties in some universities, medicine being most notorious, will admit women only up to a certain quota—usually not above 25 per cent.

Compared with other countries, the British undergraduate is younger, more specialized, and remains a student for fewer years than his transatlantic or Continental counterpart. His success rate is far higher: overall 'wastage', i.e. those who fail to complete their course, for whatever reason, averages under 14

F

per cent, compared with around 50 per cent in many Continental and American universities. This occurs as a result of the British system's degree of selectivity in demanding a certain initial level of attainment from all applicants (unlike many American 'state' universities), but possession of these qualifications does not automatically entitle the holder to a place, as in France and, until recently, in Germany. Most British students, too, differ from European and American students, both in receiving grants from the public purse, and in the level of these grants. In both Europe and the United States, it is common for students to finance themselves through part-time work. Although, in Europe, grants are available to some extent, the bulk of public support comes in the form of loans.

In addition, although many people concerned with higher education express regret that the proportion of children of manual workers at university has not altered greatly between 1939 and 1960, and between 1960 and 1970, nevertheless, in comparison with other economically advanced countries, the British percentage of around 25 per cent is better than most. This figure varies, however, from over 40 per cent at some universities, like Glasgow, to only 3 per cent at Cambridge. The Scottish proportion is higher than that for England and Wales and the major reason for the disparity would appear to be historical differences in the school educational system in the two countries, as well, perhaps, as differing working class attitudes to higher education.

One paradox, indeed, is that the upgrading of the C.A.T.s to full universities at a stroke increased the proportion of working class students in English universities. Research, however, has indicated that many able students from working class backgrounds preferred to attend C.A.T.s rather than university because they distrusted universities and felt more at ease in the technical college atmosphere and sandwich-course approach of the C.A.T.s. As, however, the C.A.T.s have shed their non-degree work, expanded their intake in numerical, social, and geographical terms, and in some cases even moved their location from crowded urban sites to green leafy traditional university surroundings (e.g. Acton to Uxbridge, Battersea to Guildford), their student population has come to resemble that of the other universities, and in this respect we seem to have taken two steps back rather than one forward.

Whatever the reasons, however, public discontent with students and student discontent with the public, or with governments, has in recent years run at a fairly high level. Within universities themselves, it was suggested in the heady days of 1968 in an article in *The Observer*[37] that university staff were afraid to be publicly quoted for fear of reprisals and that some Vice-Chancellors had taken to plotting escape routes from the feared mob. Why, then, we may ask, does the apparent distrust or misunderstanding arise?

The most simplistic explanation is summed up in the celebrated phrase 'more means worse'. Basically, the argument is that university education is about training an élite. Only a certain, and necessarily finite, percentage of any age-group is thereby fitted for benefiting from university education. Thus if university education is extended from 4 per cent of the age-group, as in 1960, to 11 per cent in 1980, the result can be only to lower standards. The puzzle is that entry qualifications of university applicants are better now than at any time in the past. Entry is more competitive than ever it was, for the simple reason that a higher proportion of every age-group is remaining at school beyond the compulsory leaving age in order to take G.C.E. or S.C.E. examinations. The 'pool of ability' case is pathetically fallacious. When only one-third of the population supply three-quarters of university entrants, clearly the pool has not been skimmed very heavily. When the two most prestigious English universities draw nearly 50 per cent of their intake from schools which serve barely 5 per cent of the population, they can hardly be held even to have access to the pool, unless, of course, the social Darwinists are right.

There is, however, a more sophisticated side to this argument. This is not that the pool of available intelligence has been fully tapped, but that only a finite proportion of an age-group are likely to gain benefit from attendance at a university. In other words, every able youngster is pressured socially, parentally and educationally into taking a degree course, whether or not he is temperamentally inclined to university life or study. The degree has become a status symbol, or a certificate of literacy or numeracy, essential for entry into a desirable career. Whereas, in the past, only those who felt an inclination for study or who sought a career in which intellectual ability was an asset, would apply. Today, as a result of social pressure, or fashion, and readily available grants, all kinds of students appear on the campus, not quite sure why they came or where they are going.

As an illustration of the attraction or compulsion of a degree, one may point to the fact that, whereas before 1960 ex-pupils of English private schools who did not gain admittance to Oxbridge decided to give university a miss (apart from a handful who took refuge in the ancient foundations at Dublin or St. Andrews). Today even the less socially attractive civic universities and ex-C.A.T.s will find a fair sprinkling of applicants from these schools. An indication of a low level of motivation has come from accusations by university teachers, particularly at some of the new universities, who have described many of their charges as dull, sullen, irresponsible and idle.

What, however, do we know of student attitudes, values, aspirations? Why do students come to university, why to a particular university, why to a particular course? Among students at Strathclyde, which is *not* typical of British universities in terms of subject balance, percentage of home residence, and social composition of students, answers to the question "What is your objective in taking your particular degree course?", have varied widely. The most common has been a vocational response, "to become a lawyer, accountant, to get a good degree, to get a decent job". But responses have ranged from "getting a better understanding of how industry works" to "because the dances are better" (than at teacher training college!).

Attitudes to the university vary from the strongly committed, who aspire to office in the students' association, to those who are enthusiastic about their sporting or academic societies, to the older student who bitterly resents compulsory membership of the students' union because when he is not studying or 'moonlighting', he wants to devote his few spare moments to his wife and children. It is, in fact, misleading to talk of 'student attitudes and values' as if they were undifferentiated and as if they applied to a homogeneous student body. It would be impossible to include the whole spectrum of values, but in the following typology we suggest that six major orientations can be identified.

First of all there exists a strong *vocational* orientation. Despite many of the high-flown phrases about the purpose of universities, the bulk of students have always attended universities to attain some useful skill or qualification. The major exceptions, as always, were the universities of Oxford and Cambridge which, until the nineteenth century, were largely finishing schools for the English upper classes. Even then, however, for the two-thirds of students who did not take degrees, the purpose was partly utilitarian, to make contact with others that would be valuable in later life. Today the plea for 'relevance' more often means 'teach me a useful skill' rather than 'let us study colonial liberation movements'. Virtually all the university teaching outside arts and pure science is directly for some intended profession, and in the arts and pure science faculties most students seek a degree as a passport to some kind of career based upon the skills they have acquired. The student who is vocationally oriented is usually too busy learning the skills of his profession to take active part in picketing factories, N.U.S. deputations, or debates. Often such students are concerned simply to pass their examinations and resent attempts to ask why a particular subject should be taught, or taught in a certain way.

Secondly, there is what may be called an *academic* category. Teachers are often accused of imagining that all their students are concerned with knowledge, with exploring the implications of any statement or discovery, that they are, in fact, mirror images of themselves. Undoubtedly, however, a proportion of students do willingly adopt academic values. There is some indication that this frequently occurs in science students, particularly in those from working class backgrounds, for whom high educational attainment means a kind of identity crisis. Unable to adhere to the values of their parents and school friends, unwilling to 'betray' their relatives by adopting a middle class, capitalistic set of values, they eschew thoughts of a career in industry and identify themselves as scientists, as best exemplified by their tutors. In addition, many students find academic work interesting and, if they find themselves being awarded high marks, undoubtedly turn their minds towards an academic career. Many others, who do not have high aspirations, but who seek what they can consider a worthwhile career such as school teaching, will also hold values which can be thought of as more academic than vocational.

Thirdly, for some students, a *social* orientation is most important. The student here sees the university as a natural staging-post between school and society and is determined to make the most of it. He rarely has this orientation without some kind of vocational or academic value being also present, but he is primarily interested in self-development. He may be found in the sports clubs, on halls committees, at any important dance. This category could, however, include those who see university experience as largely a matter of making new friends and contacts which will persist through life.

Fourthly, there are the *apathetic* students. It is argued that there are in British universities a substantial number of students who are not quite sure why they are there. They are there perhaps because their parents have persuaded them, perhaps because their school teachers indoctrinated them with the idea, but more usually, because the students have themselves chosen further education as a softer option than making up their minds about a career. They may conform outwardly to the academic rituals of essays, tutorial papers, examinations, but are likely to be easily distracted from these pursuits. The extreme version of the apathetic student is the 'drop-out' who fails his examinations, withdraws from his course, and either hangs around his former university scene, still unwilling to face the world, or withdraws to the youth 'underworld' of one of the major cities.

Fifthly, a small but important group have what we label *activist* values. This term is here intended to cover the student who has no strong commitment to his university, nor necessarily to his subject, not from lack of interest, but because he has other goals to fulfil during his student career. Basically, the term governs two types of orientation, often found together, but sometimes separate. The first orientation is what may be termed political in a broad sense, the second, equally broadly, may be described as educational. The student politician has been with us for many years. By this phrase we usually mean the student who seeks position and possibly power in a student organization. The obvious organization is the students' association or union of the university, but sometimes we are talking of someone active in a more specialist organization, often an international association of students of a particular subject. Sometimes the term may be used to describe a more conventional style of political activism. This student's main energies are devoted to furthering the cause of a particular political organization in the university and, of course, his own standing within it. Students with any of these activist leanings are usually interested in education, and hold strong views on the subject. Their orientation is, however, generally towards improving and reforming existing methods and institutions. In the recent past, their voices have aided staff who sought some element of innovation and experiment in degree structure and assessment of students. On wider issues, such as the idea of a 'comprehensive' university, their advocacy at the very minimum forces the defenders of the *status quo* or those who hold other positions on the development of universities to articulate and justify their viewpoints.

Lastly, there are those with the orientation of the *rebel*. The key word about this category is 'reject'. Whereas the apathetic student accepts passively his milieu, whereas the activist seeks either to improve it or seek compensation elsewhere, the rebel orientation rejects it without knowing quite how to replace it. Many American student rebels hold this perspective. They reject the university as they reject society and seek to destroy both. They seek fulfilment in ways as antithetical to the norms of conventional society as possible.

In Britain, however, whilst such groups exist on the fringe of youthful sub-culture, more usually the rebel student does have a ready replacement for the world in which universities, oddly, are symbols of oppression and even violence. Being almost exclusively middle class, such students see as the answer one or other variant of Marxism. The Marxist groups who articulate this orientation—usually identified by the words 'radical' or 'revolutionary'—do have rudimentary national organizations and thus can co-ordinate policies in a way that the previously described activists, on the whole, do not. Given the apathy towards student associations and councils that prevails in normal times, they frequently acquire power bases from which to irritate their own institutions, or the predominantly activist leadership of the National Union of Students (N.U.S.). In numerical terms, the rebels are a tiny minority, although their numbers may reach three figures in some institutions, but they are able to exploit any issue which may arise. Within institutions, they will seek to provoke or create reaction from university authorities, leading to martyrdom and the widening of the cause to an issue commanding wider student support.

It is, of course, mistaken, necessarily to identify a student with any one orientation. At any one moment he will probably have a mixture of two or three. Very few students who are primarily vocationally oriented will not also have some inclination towards academic or social values at some point in their courses. Equally, they may also view different parts of their university experience in different lights. Where teaching is bad, or the subject taught seems hardly relevant to his course, one may well expect the vocationally oriented student to react in a ritualistically apathetic or rebellious way.

In pointing to the complexity of the value-system of the student body, there are two points to be made. The first one is that very often the teachers present their courses in a manner likely to appeal to only one kind of student. For example, it may be said that, in general, arts and pure science courses tend to be presented in a way that appeals to the academically oriented. It has been frequently alleged that pure science courses, in particular, tend to be useful only as a training for a research career, such as is available only in the universities. In other departments, the tendency may be to teach only to the vocationally oriented. This is most true probably of medicine and related subjects, of law, and of much of engineering. The hypothesis here would be that, despite the great disparity in social origin of medical students (lowest proportion of working class students) and engineering students (highest proportion of working class students), the orientations to their course work is similar in both cases. The warning, however, is that all students may not have this orientation. This may be illustrated by engineering, where some universities, mainly ex-C.A.T.s like Loughborough, emphasize the 'practical' nature of the course, whereas in older universities like Glasgow, Belfast, and Imperial College, the approach is arguably more that of engineering science. Students, however, are not always aware of these differences when they apply for places and would-be engineering scientists might be put off by most ex-C.A.T.s, just as some 'practically-minded' might be put off by an older university. The second major point is that, in terms of academic government, the students who are most likely to be to the fore are the 'activist' or the 'rebels'. Conditions can arise which lead to a large number of normally quiescent students adopting an activist standpoint. It is important to recognize that sit-ins and the like will be brought to an end only by removing underlying conditions, not by negotiated settlements on how many students should be represented on what committees or governing bodies. The point is that constitutional amendments will give satisfaction to the small minority of activists who have a system goal of representation, in order to publicize and legitimize their activities to the mass student body. But no amount of formal consultative arrangements will affect the feelings of the majority of the students, who are normally vocationally or academically oriented, as long as library facilities remain poor, teachers appear remote or unhelpful or uninterested, grants are inadequate, and courses continue to be boring. The point is not how many student representatives ought to be on disciplinary committees, but that disciplinary procedures must be seen to be fair. The student representative in this last case is important, not for the special wisdom he may have (although in disciplinary proceedings he sometimes does), but because his presence helps to ensure that arbitrary treatment will not be meted out. The difficulty, however, is that constitutional arrangements may be seen as answering students' complaints and grievances. Staff-student committees in every department, it is argued, will ensure free communication and exchange of ideas. It can also be held, however, that a panel of teaching-oriented staff and a panel of 'activists' may illuminate certain issues but obfuscate others. The teacher's communication problem in the classroom is more often with the vocational and apathetic students and the too respectful academic ones, rather than with activists.

Given the overwhelming apathy of ordinary students to official student organizations, frequently 'rebels' oust 'activists' from office. In this event, the institution can try to educate the 'rebels' out of their basically absurd viewpoints, it can ignore them, or it can endeavour to get rid of them. The latter two courses can only be undertaken, however, if the 'rebel' orientation is confined to the miniscule minority of professional would-be revolutionaries. The rebels will not gather any substantial support from the mass of students unless they can oppose the authorities on what one commentator upon unrest on American campuses has called 'sacred topics'. In other words, an issue with a strong moral content which can command support from large numbers of students. In the United States, such an issue was the 'civil rights' movement to improve the standing of coloured Americans. In Great Britain, an example was the investment of university funds in the South African economy. Greater support can obviously be mustered if an issue, as well as having strong moral content, intimately and directly affects the lives of students. In the United States, such an issue was pre-eminently and indisputably the Vietnam war. Significantly, the most serious and most widespread unrest in Britain in recent years was due to suspicion that university files contained confidential and potentially damaging information and comments about students and their political views. As well as reflecting widespread public concern about a 'data-bank society', every student was clearly affected by his university's policy and he did have every right to know where his university stood on the issue.

The point here is that, where the 'rebel' groups have acquired a power base, the university must ensure that there is no wider issue upon which they can gather support from the mass of students who are committed in some way to the university. This can be achieved, as we have stated, not by tinkering with the constitution, but by the spirit in which university matters are tackled. Space does not permit a detailed analysis here, but such a spirit does include a commitment to educational goals, to fairness and openness in deliberations, and to taking a moral standpoint on issues like biochemical research and investment decisions.

Upon this issue, we may draw some lessons from recent American experience. Several commentators have recorded their amazement at, on the one hand, the extent of the support for radical protests in American universities in the sixties, and, on the other, the flimsiness of the pretexts for them and the sheer intellectual poverty exhibited by the leaders of these movements. The error is to suppose that the leaders, who were to an extent created by the mass media, were ever very important. The obvious truth is that in the situation of the American universities of the sixties, there was much latent discontent, which was bound to burst out in unrest at some time. There were certainly moral factors in the disturbances. Many students wished to help the American Negro to attain full citizenship of the Republic, many were offended by the material excesses of private affluence, by American military and financial imperialism, and by many other unpleasant faces of American society. But closer to the campus there were three issues which served to make unrest inevitable.

To begin with, Clark Kerr predicted in 1963[38] that the growth of the mega-campus was placing intolerable strains upon the fabric of the American university. He then described the 'multiversity' but did not necessarily endorse it, and he could see that growth, which glorified research at the expense of undergraduate teaching, was building up to an explosion. Secondly, connected with this was an apparent change in values among staff and administrators. Large research programmes funded by sources over which the university authorities had no control, mainly federal government agencies, had shifted the balance of power away from undergraduate teaching departments, hitherto the core of the traditional university, into the hands of the research entrepreneurs. That this process, "the degradation of the academic dogma", as Robert Nisbet has described it,[39] would ultimately cause an outburst from those suffering most, the students, always seemed probable. Above all, there was the Vietnam war, and the draft. Entry to college or university postponed call-up, but failure to proceed on one's course (and American failure rates average around 50 per cent) meant for many students, enlistment in a futile war in which eventually over 50,000 Americans died. Moral and political concern at American policy and practice in South-East Asia was present in a large degree, but it would be only realistic to recognize the timeless truth of Rod McKuen's song that:

> "Soldiers who want to be heroes
> Number practically zero,
> But there are millions,
> Who want to be civilians."

In 1973, American campuses are relatively peaceful. It may be that students are a fickle lot and that a new generation has different, or more traditional priorities. However, it seems simpler to observe that the Vietnam issue has been defused, the draft is being phased out, and, with a national cut-back in research expenditure, power on the campus is returning to the undergraduate department, with a substantial teaching commitment. The large campus still exists, but that alone is not issue enough for outrage.

In Great Britain, few of these conditions have been present. By American standards, British institutions are still small, research does not displace teaching, and there has been nothing comparable to the Vietnam war and the draft. Consequently, there has not been a substansive issue to involve to any great extent the great majority of British students. Moral issues have been few, the 'political files' and 'South African investment' being the only two to have greater than local relevance. The great bulk of students have no interest in the pseudo-Marxism of the 'rebels'. The students who matter are those working for a meaningful qualification or who seek to gain greater understanding of their subject or their world. They are the ones who will make or break student 'revolts' and it is to their interests and aspirations that universities should direct their instruction. Student government is usually well served by those whom we have termed the 'activists', and, while it does no harm for the senior members of a university to explain themselves to this usually articulate and well-intentioned group of students, their importance should be kept in perspective. The lesson of recent disturbances is that universities must pay attention to the working and living conditions of students and to the spirit in which student grievances are tackled. Few doubt, for example, that present standards of teaching could be improved, although without some conscious goal-oriented programme, as outlined earlier, we doubt if they will be.

Administrators

In the traditional concept of the university, the administrator has no place. He is not a member. He is not *civis universitatis,* as is the newly matriculated 'fresher'. In a community model, administration is carried out by a senior teacher in a few spare hours. For routine and humdrum work, the scholars may hire lowly clerks. Until recently, such was the scale and scope of university administration that this model was not entirely inappropriate. Such administration as existed was conducted at a leisurely pace, in a gentlemanly manner. The sixties put an end to all that. Growth and complexity meant the end of easy informal arrangements and everywhere the process known to the social scientist as bureaucratization, has bloomed. Tight budgeting and the co-ordinating of the requirements of large and growing departments have entailed the development of a planning, co-ordinative and even controlling function upon every campus. Whilst academic staff usually affect to regard administrators as unnecessary, many have, none the less, welcomed this process of bureaucratization. Despite its unpopular import to the general public, bureaucratization means no more than the establishment of standards, rules, and criteria which are applied to all equally. The older, informal approach, which the social scientist would call 'patrimonial', too often meant that favour accrued to those able to influence the vice-chancellor.

There does, however, appear to be evidence that the administrative staff grew more than in proportion to the growth of the institution. Increased size means greater problems of co-ordination. More specialists possessing forms of expertise relatively new to university administration have to be hired. This is not a process peculiar to universities. Industry has known for many years that size brings problems of co-ordination and control. In a university, scope for operating economies of any kind is extremely limited, and the point of increasing overhead charges comes very early.

At the head of a university's administrative system is the Vice-Chancellor (Principal in Scotland). His position is unique, for he is both the supreme academic and administrative officer. On the one hand, he is the key figure as chairman of the Senate, and, by virtue of his *ex officio* membership of every important academic committee, the sole potential co-ordinator of all things academic. On the other hand, he is the executive head of the administrative hierarchy over whom he has direct control. The Vice-Chancellor is by far the most important figure in the university. The Robbins Committee, even in 1963, noted that "no other enterprise would impose on its chairman the variety and burden of work that the modern university requires of its vice-chancellor", and that "the needs of expansion and the increasingly complex relations between institutions of higher education and government will impose upon the heads of universities a quite insupportable burden, unless steps are taken to relieve them".[40]

His American equivalent, the university President, Clark Kerr described as a many-faced character. "He is expected to be a friend of the students, a colleague of the faculty (academic staff), a good fellow with the *alumni* (former students), a sound administrator with the trustees, a good speaker with the public, an astute bargainer with the foundations and federal agencies, a politician with the state legislature, a friend of industry, labour, and agriculture, a persuasive diplomat with donors, a champion of education generally, a supporter of the professions (particularly law and medicine), a spokesman to the Press, a scholar in his own right, a public servant at the state and national levels, a devotee of opera and football equally, a decent human being, a good husband and father, an active member of a church. Above all, he must enjoy travelling in airplanes, eating his meals in public, and attending public ceremonies."[41]

In the past, most noteworthy vice-chancellors have been strong, usually authoritarian characters. This is less likely today. Only in the new universities of the sixties have vice-chancellors been able to guide their universities along the paths desired by them, since it was they who appointed the key foundation staff and who were largely responsible for planning the growth and character of their institutions. Even there, however, their powers are circumscribed, both by the power of public and parliamentary opinion and by the constitutional framework of the university. Some have argued that real power in the university is so diffused that the influence of any one person or position is limited. Certainly, in one case where a substantial proportion of the senate reacted overtly against the apparent wishes of the Vice-Chancellor, as happened at Warwick in 1968, the result was a change of direction by the Vice-Chancellor.

There was a time when some academic staff moved over fairly easily to administrative positions, but the days of this amateurism have passed and academic administration is becoming increasingly a profession in its own right. It is important, however, to distinguish between the administrators who are concerned almost entirely with the academic business of the university and who, therefore, work closely with academic staff, and the 'technical specialists', like architects and computer staff, who apply their special skills to areas of university activity and who do not usually come into close touch with the academic staff. The paradox is that the university administrator's main job is to help the academics achieve the research, teaching, or social goals of the university. Jacques Barzun defends administrators by asking academics, "Do you want to bring your own chalk into the classroom? The administrator's job is to see that the chalk is there."[42] The administrator has an auxiliary role. Indeed, many administrators in Britain consciously see themselves as a civil service of universities, advising, serving and executing for academic bodies as civil servants do for ministers. Yet, it is they who have the overtly managerial orientation. They are more committed to the individual institution as an institution than the academics who increasingly see their loyalty and advancement in terms of their discipline rather than of their university.

In many respects, the university administrator resembles the hospital administrator. Both work in organizations, the main goals of which are achieved by a professional group. Both are more administratively oriented to the institution than their professional masters, and both share the frustration of trying vainly to get medicals or academics to raise administrative procedures from the lowest priority position. Yet there is an important difference. Among the medical personnel of a hospital there is greater homogeneity of outlook and greater professional cohesion than among the widely varied academic staff of a university. If we accept that the appropriate perspective with which to view universities is a pluralistic one (Chapter 1), then it follows that the role of the mediator is an important one. Given the scarcity of resources available to universities, from the late sixties onwards, some kind of arbitration rather than mediation becomes essential. In such a situation, the centrally-placed administrator who can operate a small planning unit, and who has thus greater knowledge of the overall position than all but a handful of academic staff, is in a powerful position. In the hospital, the secretary and his staff will tend to lose any argument because of the relative unanimity of the medical viewpoint and also because of the much greater relative disparity in both social status and financial reward between senior medical personnel and senior administrative staff. By contrast, engineers and social scientists are far less likely to close ranks against administrative demands. Moreover, there is substantial parity in terms of financial reward, and, increasingly, of social esteem between academic staff and administrators.

Wiser administrators have recognized, however, the way in which their role has developed into a planning and policy-forming one, and warn that conflict between academic staff and administrators is likely unless great care is taken. We would argue that greater understanding between academics and administrators is sorely needed, though few universities seem to recognize the fact. Improved communications and better interpersonal relations will improve matters, but of themselves are not enough. The answer appears to be for university government to be reconstructed in such a way that academic bodies are better able to exercise a decision-making capacity.

CHAPTER 6

Universities and their Environment

Until this point, we have been discussing universities as if they were closed systems. In some ways this is appropriate. There exists a widespread view that universities are remote from the communities in which they exist. Within universities, many staff have a predisposition to use phrases like 'out there in the real world', and to assume that somehow what goes on in universities is less 'real' than similar phenomena elsewhere. It is perhaps understandable that those, especially on the smaller residential campuses, finding themselves caught up in the minutiae and trivia that are typical of life in a small enclosed society, will somehow imagine that 'the grass is greener' on the other side of the walls. Perhaps it is a defect of a university career that those following it often have little experience of organizations outside the teaching or research worlds. If they had, they would recognize that only a tiny percentage of the employees of industrial firms, or of public organizations, have any contact with or awareness of, their organization's external environment. For the mass of participants, life in most large organizations tends to be enclosed, insulated and often frustrating.

But there does remain the impression that universities, perhaps unconsciously, cultivate this impression of remoteness from everyday affairs. If so, the reason can be found in one of the less pleasant legacies left to all our present institutions by the ancient universities of England: the tradition of monasticism and scholarly contemplation with which they have in the past been associated, and which they have not yet entirely abandoned. There is ample evidence that for the bulk of their

G

history, England's ancient universities were irrelevant reactionary seminaries, whose degrees were taken only by a minority of serious scholars. Indeed, a series of Royal Commissions were required in the nineteenth century to drag them out of the seventeenth century and most of the improvements in English university education have occurred despite, rather than because of, them. Every other university in England, with the exception of Durham, founded in the nineteenth century, was established largely to compensate for the shortcomings of the ancient institutions. Most were founded with industrialists' or local authority money and were explicitly intended to serve local and commercial interests. The 'lay' members on their governing bodies were there largely to ensure that this course was followed.

Today, there can be no doubt that universities are open to the influence of their environment to a marked degree. We have remarked that an important 'system' goal of universities is to preserve their traditional independence. Nevertheless, because they depend upon public funds from one source or another for all but a tiny proportion of their income, they are highly sensitive to public criticism. Many universities have in the past decade appointed information officers or public relations consultants to foster a wider awareness of their socially relevant activities. In general terms, there would be wide agreement that the universities have done all that was asked of them by governments in expanding to accommodate the higher number of school-leavers seeking university places. In terms of research activity, curriculum revision, and intellectual training, there are, of course, variations in response. By and large, the ex-C.A.T.s have shown greater willingness—they mostly had greater opportunity—to gear their activities, on a 'service station' model, to the needs of clients. In terms of response by subject area, engineering and business faculties, being concerned with 'practical' matters, have shown greater concern than pure science or arts faculties, but the latter two have hardly been laggard. Courses which have appeared in recent years, in environmental engineering, urban studies, pollution control, operational research and now 'total technology' hardly indicate that university response lags far behind public need.

The university comes into contact with many 'publics'. The

most important of these are central government and its various agencies, Parliament, local authorities and communities, industrial and commercial firms, schools, and the Press and broadcasting organizations which affect the viewpoint of the public at large. The universities are presented to the general public mainly through the mass media. Students tend to be prominent in demonstrations or in association with causes, such as strikes, which are unpopular with large sections of the public. There is, therefore, an awareness of the need to publicize that work of the university that contributes to the public good. This tends to take the form of publicizing the products of research programmes, such as the Aston-discovered plastics which disintegrate after prolonged exposure to ultra-violet light (sunlight). In addition, most universities are hypersensitive to public criticism and will, therefore, go to great lengths to satisfy complainants.

The schools are the source of the universities' main input, the students, and one might expect considerable communication to take place with them. Those universities which have a substantial intake from their own region, mainly, in effect, the Scottish universities, maintain a substantial liaison with the schools. However, the intake of most English universities is usually from such a diffuse range of sources that individual contacts between schools and universities are difficult. In both countries, however, the effects of schools upon universities are almost non-existent, whereas the effects of universities upon schools, mainly through their admissions policies, are immense. The commitments of most universities in England to the three years' narrowly-specialized Honours degree is a major causal factor in the absurdly early specialization in English schools, and a major barrier to any broadening of school curricula. An outstanding example of university attitudes is that of Oxford and Cambridge, who insist upon retaining their own entrance examinations. If their wish to broaden the social composition of their intake is sincere, they should recognize that their policy in effect demands that every school in the country has its curriculum dictated by them.

At the other end of the university production process, the professions and industry and commerce are the potential employers of the graduates. In the case of medicine and, to a lesser extent, law, the professions have great influence. Professional bodies validate the courses of the institutions which offer them. The same is true to a lesser extent of architecture, accountancy, and many engineering courses. The influence of industrial firms is more indirect, but their recruitment policies do affect academic development. The expansion of economics departments in the sixties was affected partly by the comparative ease with which economics graduates could find employment. In research, industry's influence is more direct. Most departments welcome research sponsored by industrial firms. In addition, firms are often encouraged to use university equipment and staff expertise on a commercial basis.

There is, of course, one viewpoint which wholly approves of universities being involved with industry. There has, however, been a contrary view, that overdue dependence upon industry for research funding can distort the academic development of a department. The main argument of some influential academic staff and many students at Warwick University in 1968 was that the Vice-Chancellor had so zealously courted industrial wealth and influence that he had displaced the proper purpose of the university. In 1973, J. A. G. Griffith, Professor of Public Law at London University, protested that Queen Mary College, University of London, should not accept the endowment of a Chair of Credit Law by the Finance Houses Association. Writing with Professor R. H. Hilton on behalf of the Council for Academic Freedom and Democracy, he declared as a general principle their doubt "whether any college or university should accept an endowment from any private, commercial or industrial organization which has a direct interest in the subject matter of the post to be created, especially when the subject matter is a highly controversial activity with strong social, political, and economic implications".[43] In these and other cases, allegations were made that the 'academic freedom' of individuals and institutions was being infringed by allowing industry this direct stake in the university.

Another area of involvement with industry which has caused controversy is that of the activities of university-owned consultancy companies. More universities are establishing these as a way of bringing order to staff consultancy projects, as well as to raise revenue, but there are those who argue persuasively that effort and resources are diverted by this process, and the integrity of the university infringed. This was the argument of those operational research staff at Sussex University who successfully opposed a proposal to set up a limited liability company with Lancaster University to attract income for consultancy and research in their field. As one put it, they had to break "a vicious circle in which the need for a regular income from industry got a stranglehold on both our research and our teaching".[44]

With local authorities, universities have two kinds of contact. In the first case, representatives of local authorities sit on governing bodies and local authorities often contribute to the university funds from their rates income. In the early days of the provincial universities, this could represent a substantial proportion of their income, but today there are only a few institutions for which it represents more than one per cent of total income. Oddly, however, two universities who, some allege, have overreacted to student disturbances, Essex and Stirling, both get an unusually high proportion of their income (seven and eight per cent respectively) from local authorities, and would have problems if these funds were cut off, as is threatened from time to time. The other contact with local authorities which universities cannot avoid is in obtaining planning consent for their expansion. In city-centre sites, where the rates income from educational buildings is a great deal less than that which could be obtained from office blocks or other commercial development, city councils may not be particularly co-operative. Early in 1973 a report by a panel of inquiry into the Greater London Development plan recommended that an attempt be made to transfer existing universities and colleges out of London to less crowded areas, in order to ease pressure on housing and other developments.

Studies of the economic impact of universities on smaller communities show a somewhat contrary effect. Studies of the economic relationship between university and town in St. Andrews, Stirling and Exeter[45] indicate the important contribution they make to the local economy. In the most recent study of Exeter, a city of some 80,000 people, the researchers, Lewes and Kirkness, indicate that in 1970/71 the university, with 3,387 students and 390 academics, contributed 4.2 per cent of the city council's total rates revenue, and that the gross incomes of university employees and students was almost £4 million.[46] In their input-output study of St. Andrews, with a population of 10,000, the university with 1,822 students and 246 academic staff at the time, Blake and McDowell concluded that the university was three times as beneficial to the town, in terms of pounds of household income generated per £100 expenditure, than the local economy's only other major input, tourism. Any apparently marginal excessive cost in the country's higher education budget attributable to the smaller universities, would appear to be more than offset by the high social benefit and the relatively low opportunity cost of siting new university colleges in smaller towns in the less prosperous regions.

The most important figure, however, in every university's environment is its major paymaster, the government. The government supports the universities in three ways, by paying students maintenance grants, by supporting research and graduate study through the research councils, and by direct payments to the institutions through the University Grants Committee, the Exchequer grants, as they are called in the accounts. Our main concern is with government-university relations through the medium of the U.G.C. The question of student maintenance grants involves the universities as institutions only indirectly, as when students refuse to pay increased fees for halls of residence as part of a campaign to have grants increased. Likewise, relationships with the research councils tend to involve individuals and departments rather than the university. The councils are, however, the biggest single source of research funds, and government policy concerning them can touch the universities' rawest nerve.

The Committee, which is composed mainly of university personnel acting in an individual capacity, stands between the universities and the government. The universities individually send their plans and requests to the U.G.C. which collates them and negotiates with the Government on the total sum to be allocated. The committee then disburses the money to the various institutions. The government, therefore, is able to control the overall rate of growth of the universities without getting involved in any academic decisions. Thus, it is argued, the universities retain their cherished institutional freedom. It is this autonomy which marks the universities off from the rest of the higher education system. University governing bodies are responsible to no one for the policies they pursue. Although outside interests are represented on the governing bodies, the persons who hold positions on them, even when they do so by virtue of their public office (e.g. a Lord Mayor or Lord Provost of a city), act in an individual capacity.

The accounts of each university, and of the U.G.C., have since 1970 been open to inspection by the Comptroller and Auditor General. The Comptroller, however, is not a government servant. He is the chief officer of the House of Commons Public Accounts Committee, by convention now chaired by a senior Opposition member. The Comptroller's Office does not question whether or not a policy is right or wrong, but asks only that funds are properly accounted for and that no malpractices occur.

But it is, in theory, up to each university to decide how it uses most of the resources allocated to it by the U.G.C. It may, if it chooses, decline to develop studies in certain fields, or it may limit its growth in order to retain a special characteristic. Keele University in the sixties could probably have grown faster, had it not preferred to retain its character as a residential university, rather than develop its academic facilities ahead of its residential ones. Currently there is a debate going on in the University of Wales as to whether it should expand at all. One plan calls for expansion from the present 13,000 students to 27,000 in 1981/2. Since Wales supplies only 11,000 university students at present, such expansion would inevitably eradicate the national character of the Welsh colleges. At the moment only some 43 per cent of all students of the University of Wales are Welsh, compared with 82 per cent in the early fifties. Some feel that the main priority should be in retaining or restoring a Welsh identity rather than expansion.

Similar fears are from time to time expressed about the admissions policies of some of the Scottish universities, notably Edinburgh, Dundee and St. Andrew's. In Scotland there is one viewpoint which claims that the Scottish universities would be better served by being taken out of the U.G.C.'s list and being made accountable to the Secretary of State for

Scotland, who is responsible for all other education in Scotland. A university may decline to expand in certain areas if this is going to affect its special characteristics. In the present climate of student demand and government outlook, many of the 'technological' universities could expand their business, social sciences or arts departments at a faster rate than their science and engineering departments. Some decline to do so, since they place great store in remaining 'technological', i.e. engineering-dominated, institutions.

There must, however, be some doubts as to whether institutional freedom from government control is in fact guaranteed by the present arrangements. The Robbins committee suggested that five essential freedoms had to exist if there was to be proper 'academic freedom' in the institutional sense.[47] These were staff appointments and dismissals, the admission and examination of students, the curricula and standards of the courses, the balance between teaching and research and freedom of development. In terms of the fourth freedom, the balance between teaching and research, most university staff would insist that freedom to choose what research to pursue should be also made explicit. This last point clearly affects the attitude of those members of staff discussed earlier who are worried about the effects of business-sponsored research upon the balance and development of their university.

In terms of staff appointments and dismissals, admission of students, curricula and standards of courses, it is not doubted that governmental interference with university autonomy is very slight, if it exists at all. As to staff, overall salary scales and the overall proportion of senior grades is decided by government, but unlike many other countries, there is no way for any outside body to interfere with appointments. This is only one of the many rights taken for granted in Great Britain which is absent in many parts of the world. Even in Western Europe, it is common for appointments to be formally confirmed by central or state governments, and even in the United States, some state authorities, most notably those in California, have intervened in appointment matters.

No central body vets university courses or degrees of any kind. This is only one of the many differences between universities and polytechnics. In the latter, departments have to complete an exhausting obstacle race before a course is finally approved by the Council for National Academic Awards. The Robbins Committee argued that the incentive to get a high place in public esteem is sufficient safeguard against a decline in university standards. In addition, the appointment of external examiners from other universities for all but introductory degree courses ensures a substantial degree of uniformity of standards. Nevertheless, there are those who would argue that some greater element of co-ordination would do no harm.

There is no doubt that it is easier to get a 'good' degree classification in a given subject in some universities than in others. Between different subject areas there are wide variations in awards. For example, it is five or six times as easy to get a first class degree in a technology subject for which there is little competition for places, than it is in a social science subject, where the competition for places is intense.

With regard to the remaining two areas of institutional freedom—the balance between teaching and research, and freedom of development—there has been increasing disquiet among university staff and administrators. Ever since Sir John Wolfenden, then chairman of the U.G.C., announced the finance to be made available from 1967–1972, pressure has been applied to universities to concentrate more upon undergraduate teaching and less upon graduate work, which usually involves research. Not only was this tendency reinforced when the 1972–77 plans were announced by the Department of Education and Science, but the overall ratio of students to staff was to be allowed to worsen from 1:8 to 1:10. The only possible interpretation of this proposal is that staff are to spend more time on teaching and less on research. The merits of the proposal are open to debate, but this is certainly a decision of the government, not of the universities.

Further anxiety about the continued autonomy of universities to follow research of their own choosing has resulted from the proposal that the government contributions to the research councils, which in turn distribute money to those research proposals they judge to be most fruitful, should be lessened. Instead, the proposal from the Central Policy Review Staff, welcomed by the government, is that government departments be encouraged to make direct agreements with universities for them to conduct research into topics of direct interest and relevance to them. The intention, of course, was to shift more emphasis and resources to applied research rather than pure or basic research.

It is, however, the last of the Robbins committee's five freedoms, that of development, that is most difficult to detect today. To explain why this is so, it is perhaps helpful to indicate how funds are distributed to the universities by the U.G.C.

Grants from the U.G.C. are basically of four types, recurrent grants to cover normal running costs and maintenance, non-recurrent grants for items such as new buildings, equipment grants for scientific and technical equipment and earmarked grants to encourage specific academic developments, given over and above the general recurrent grant.

By far the most important is the recurrent grant which covers all normal running costs. This includes salaries of teaching and research staff, by far the largest single item, maintenance of buildings and rates, administration, salaries of technicians and laboratory assistants, some research grants and central services such as libraries and computers. In theory, each university has control over how it spends the grant. In practice, these grants are made only after lengthy discussion between each university and U.G.C. representatives over planned developments. Informally, the U.G.C. makes it plain what it wishes to encourage and what it does not.

Moreover, new academic development invariably means expansion of physical resources, new or extended premises, additional furnishings, new technical equipment. Provided it approves of the purpose of the expenditure and provided that the costs do not exceed certain limits, the U.G.C. will provide a once-for-all capital grant. This grant will go, in whole or in part, towards the building work, professional fees, furniture and site and property purchases. The itemised costs of these can break down to quite small amounts, even to the costs of individual items of furniture, and demand formidable control procedures on the part of the university. Because of its control of new buildings expenditure, the U.G.C. can effectively control the broad path of a university's development.

In addition to the new building controls, the U.G.C. can also exert influence through grants for scientific equipment, whether in new or existing buildings. This form of grant was introduced in 1968/69 to cover university requirements for all scientific equipment. In essence, the U.G.C. allocates each university a total sum for equipment for each quinquennium. During each year of the quinquennium they can draw upon this grant up to a maximum amount. They can, however, carry over amount still unspent into later years. Lastly, the 'earmarked' grant is a category for encouraging specific developments, such as expanding medical schools or for improving library stocks. It is not often used. In 1967–72 it was used to encourage business and management education in certain universities, and in 1972–77, it is being used for medical education. However, very often, as we have indicated the 'recurrent' grant often contains an informal element of 'earmarking'.

At the beginning of each quinquennium, the Committee issues statements of their broad intentions. For instance, they have stated that currently they are not encouraging new schools of architecture, new schools of law, or new departments or addition.l degree courses in a new language. They make it clear that they want to see the student: staff ratio in the social sciences improve from 11 to about 10.5 at a time when the overall average is moving from 8 to 10. U.G.C. directions are, however, not always as general. In 1971/72, the U.G.C., with plans for the next quinquennium in mind, first suspended and then modified existing plans to expand science places. Three universities, Loughborough, University College, Swansea, and Salford, whose building plans had not been finally approved, were prevented from carrying out their plans. Loughborough had sought to expand its capacity in physics and engineering, but was told that this could not happen because there were unfilled places in these subjects elsewhere. This decision means that a university which attracts science students is unable to expand or to start new courses without reducing numbers on existing ones. Conversely, the unsuccessful universities have an incentive to innovate, in order to fill their spare capacity. Thus, it can be argued, success is penalized.

There is clearly no easy answer to this problem, but it is one likely to stay with us for a while, since uniformity of attraction and achievement is increasingly unlikely in a system of some eighty university institutions. National planning is likely to be arbitrary and to be based on overall physical factors rather than on encouraging a more open, market-style, system. The U.G.C. or Department of Education and Science are unlikely to attempt any qualitative judgements, but will seek safety in impersonal numbers and ratios. Assuming, however, that higher education continues to be a 'consumption' commodity, one that should be available to anyone willing and qualified to undertake it, there is one obvious 'solution' to the problem, a solution indicated by the Robbins Committee some ten years ago. University fees now contribute a derisory eight per cent to total income. Since most of these are paid by the government anyway, there seems little reason why these cannot be raised to a level that more properly reflects teaching costs. The fees for all British students could then be automatically paid in full by the Exchequer. For those who at present do not qualify even for the minimum grant some generous scholarship, rebate, or loan scheme could be devised. There is no obvious economic, social or administrative reason why this could not be implemented. Alas, there are few known examples where politicians or civil servants have voluntarily relinquished control over any important resource.

It appears to many that the U.G.C. now merely puts an acceptable face upon a broad policy decided in Whitehall. It co-ordinates the university submissions to the government and, no doubt, does a conscientious job in distributing the Exchequer grants. Nevertheless, there are those who wonder whether or not the Committee of Vice-Chancellors and Principals is not the proper body to co-ordinate university planning in this country. It can then confront the Department of Education and Science (D.E.S.), if necessary and thereby force open discussion and justification of government policy. As it is, the Committee of Vice-Chancellors is increasingly taking a direct path to the D.E.S.; it may not be long until they walk it alone.

CHAPTER 7

Control and Effectiveness

As we have suggested previously, some element of control in any organization is essential, if progress is to be made towards achieving the goals of the organization. In hierarchical organizations, the structure of organization itself provides the means of control. Each manager or administrator supervises the work of his subordinates and keeps a close enough watch on their activities to ensure that the organization's objectives are being followed. He in turn is closely supervised by his superior. In the university, however, we have noticed that there is a comparative absence of hierarchy. Moreover, the orientation of most staff is 'professional', which implicitly rejects hierarchical organization as relevant for their work. In common with most 'professional' organizations there is an absence of sanctions. As with doctors, sexual immorality is a surer ground for dismissal than incompetence, and not since a celebrated case in the 1930s has there been a serious attempt to declare a professor redundant. As in most organizations, promotion or transfer sideways to an advisory rather than executive role is the means of removal.

With students, also, there is no graduated system of hierarchically imposed controls, especially as far as discipline is concerned. An extreme example was the case of the University of Essex, where the Vice-Chancellor, Dr. A. E. Sloman, having the apparently reasonable belief that if you treat students like adults they will behave like adults, created almost no rules for students. The responsibility for discipline was largely left to the students themselves. When, in 1967, some students showed their displeasure at a speaker from the chemical and biological warfare research establishment at Porton Down, by pouring mustard powder over him and disrupting his lecture, the absence of a disciplinary code meant that the only power the university could use was the Vice-Chancellor's right to suspend any student without giving a reason. In academic matters, control over a student is only slightly less extreme. The one effective sanction a department has over a student who does not submit work in time, or does not appear at tutorials or laboratories, is to exclude him from degree examinations in that subject. Because of understandable reluctance to invoke this sanction, a great deal of lead-swinging is often tolerated.

The main control method used in universities is basically a form of self-control based upon selection and commitment. Relatively few students fail to gain a qualification at British universities, because before they are admitted they must have attained a considerable level of academic competence at school or elsewhere. Thus, in general, nearly all students admitted to a given course are thought to have the ability to complete it. There is no 'weeding out' process in the first term, as frequently occurs in American universities. Moreover, in order to attain university entrance qualifications on leaving school, students will already have displayed a high level of commitment. They will often have stayed at home studying while their contemporaries may have been enjoying economic freedom and a variety of leisure pursuits. Within the university, the committed student, expected to exhibit self-discipline, is subjected to control through assessment of his work in term essays and exams. These feed back to the student information about his performance. It is up to him to do something about it. He will rarely be reprimanded and never punished for poor class-work. Usually, teaching staff do not seek out those whose work is below standard. At most, a general warning is issued and it is up to the student to ask for help from his tutor or other member of the staff. To a lesser extent, class performance and degree examination results do act as a control for staff. If the overall results are usually poor, and this is noticed, the reasons will be investigated. There could be a revision of teaching methods or a change of personnel.

As far as staff are concerned, the university relies even more upon selection and commitment. Once given a permanent appointment, in most universities, a teacher has almost total job security. He is on a fixed salary scale and cannot be motivated to better performance by the promise of additional financial rewards. He will perform well if he is committed to his work, if he values recognition of his worth by his colleagues or his students, or if he seeks professional advancement. No university authority has control over the presence or absence of these factors. Since the university as an institution has little control over the work of its senior members, the recruitment and selection procedures become very important. There is widespread agreement that in selecting and promoting staff, research-performance and productivity are more important than evidence of teaching ability. In making appointments, the selectors rely on four sources of information. These are confidential reports from referees, an interview with the candidate that rarely exceeds thirty minutes, evidence of degree performance, and publications. It is usually easier to evaluate the latter two criteria more 'objectively' and thus they carry greater weight. Recent research[48] has indicated that candidates who apply for a post in the university where they took their degree stand a much better chance than candidates who took their degree elsewhere (apart from those who took their degree at Oxford and Cambridge). This suggests that where selectors can have reliable information about other qualities desired in a candidate, this will lead to such candidates being favoured. Nevertheless, while the evidence available suggests that universities seek quality first—the quality of one's first degree appears to be the most important single factor influencing appointment—they have very little information about the degree of commitment a candidate may have to teaching, research, or to the institution.

We have seen, then, that university authorities have very little formal control over the activities of individual members of staff. In departments which use substantial laboratory equipment, heads can enforce compliance to some extent by controlling access to these facilities. However, especially in larger departments, the professor will not be able to influence subordinates to pursue the goals he desires unless they too are committed to them. The most obvious way to obtain that commitment, the literature of social science tells us, is by involving them in the goal-setting process, and by obtaining their aid in monitoring progress towards the desired goal. At faculty or senate level, the same is true. If academic objectives are desired, the nature of the control process is such that those on whose efforts attainment of the goal depends must take part in the goal-setting process, at the level at which it affects them. Overall co-ordination can be achieved only through a body in which the staff have confidence, which means a body in which their interest is effectively represented. In terms of relationships of depart-ments to more central authorities, we have indicated that very little academic control can be exercised. In terms, however, of access to physical resources, it can be argued that control by the central authorities can be substantial. As a result of the scarcity of resources, and of the need to account clearly for expenditure, departments everywhere have had to become ac-customed to budgetary devices of various kinds controlling expenditure under separate categories. Physical planning and control of expenditure is now a major feature of university organization and an obvious source of friction between administrators and academic staff.

For control of the main outputs, graduates and knowledge, universities depend upon the strength of the value-system of the teachers, particularly of the professors. This feature, as we noted earlier, is the hall-mark of the 'professional' as opposed to the 'bureaucratic' organization. The strength of shared values as a cohesive force was indicated by one of the earliest attempts to formulate 'principles' of management. In the 1930s, Mooney and Reiley referred to the "power of doctrine" which allowed the Pope to supervise directly the work of upwards of two thousand bishops.[49] To a management theorist schooled in bureaucratic principles, such a "span of control" was ridiculous. It could work, however, in the Roman Catholic Church, because there was virtual unanimity of view about the goals and methods of the organization. It would be fascinating to hear Mooney and Reiley's view of the 'power of doctrine' today, given that the degree of unanimity on methods of that organization has lessened in the past forty years.

There is ample evidence for doubting substantial unanimity of view about the purposes or methods of universities, even in a society as homogeneous as that as Great Britain. Our evidence would include variations in the standards of degrees awarded, both between different faculties and among all faculties in different institutions, and the different quality-goals expressed in different disciplines and universities. Given the substantial degree of mutual incomprehension which exists between sociologists and chemists, between mechanical engineers and philosophers, between accountants and botanists, it would be strange indeed if there were to be a substantial amount of agreement on the purposes of the university.

The advantages of the 'pluralistic' model of the university, as typified in the 'multiversity', is that it suggests how cohesion is maintained in the absence of agreement about purposes or methods. By apathy. The secret is to grant autonomy to faculties and departments 'to do their own thing'. This is a negative version of what some consider the main motive force in the American Congress, the phenomenon of 'log rolling' or 'you scratch my back, and I'll scratch yours'. Because of autonomy, there is no incentive for anyone to change anything. What makes universities pleasant places to work in is that if one disagrees with certain policies of one's department, faculty or institution, the obvious course is not to attempt to change matters, but simply to withdraw to 'cultivate one's own garden'. Thus, as we suggested in Chapter 3, when the major academic decision-making body is composed mainly of every professor representing every vested interest in the university, scope for innovation of any kind is limited.

We implied earlier, however, that universities will somehow have to settle their identity crisis and be more certain of their goals if they are to be effective in the 1980s. How can this be achieved? By a return to authoritarianism? Baldridge's study of New York University indicated that where drastic changes were essential to the continued survival of the institution, power was a major factor in determining the outcome. But we would suggest another way. Studies of organizations with a good record of innovation suggest that the best way to plan and implement changes is not through authoritarian methods, but in forming collaborative problem-solving and decision-taking groups which set the objectives, devise the operational plans and control their implementation. Groups of this kind, existing at various levels in a university, could establish conscious goal-oriented programmes in all relevant areas of activity.

H

Such a process, as we suggested in Chapter 2, has to involve an evaluation of the degree of success of the programme. This may include an element of measurement of performance, which in any organization is not a venture to be undertaken lightly. In industry, over-concern for measurement has often led to gross distortion of effort when managers endeavour to make certain that their record in the terms used to measure performance meets the required standards, at the expense of other factors which, in the long run, are going to have as much effect. When policemen used to spend the second-last day of every month issuing parking 'tickets' in order to raise the number of convictions, neither police morale nor public goodwill towards them was greatly improved. When combat units in Vietnam were evaluated on the number of enemy confirmed killed, there was little incentive to take prisoners for interrogation, or to distinguish between enemy and neutral or friendly civilians when it came to a body count. It is important that the process of measurement be kept in perspective. In talking about achieving goals or objectives, it is implied that lack of achievement means failure in some absolute sense. Goals, however, we suggested earlier, sometimes are most usefully seen as ideals, towards which one strives, rather than operational objectives. In this sense, few organizations ever achieve their goals completely. It would be misleading to suggest that most organizations are completely ineffective. What matters is the organization's comparative effectiveness, both against its own effectiveness in the past, and against that of similarly-placed organizations.

It is this reasoning which lay behind Peter Drucker's insistence in his *Practice of Management* that the use of 'profit' alone as a criterion of performance for the business enterprise was a false and irrelevant exercise. Profit, even if clearly defined in order that like was truly compared with like, was only one of several indicators of performance. Other criteria included both quantifiable measures, such as percentage share of the market for a given product, and unquantifiable measures, like the state of development, training and potential of management. Similarly, in universities, no single measure can give a criterion, in either an absolute or comparative sense. A combination of many, however, may give some impression of performance compared with other institutions. Using a comprehensive set of measures, performance in British universities may be compared with those in comparable countries.

When discussing, for instance, the costs of higher education, it is not enough to use absolute figures such as expenditure per student, for the simple reason that the annual cost expenditure per student of medicine is a much greater figure than that for an arts student. That is one of the factors that has to be considered when costs of polytechnics and universities are being compared. An additional point in the same vein is that even international expenditure per student is misleading, since most American and Continental universities contain a far larger proportion of students who will not succeed in obtaining a qualification. Cost per graduate is the relevant indicator. Politicians and others who complain about the proportion of national expenditure devoted to higher education, and about the amount it costs to educate apparently ungrateful students, have very little to tell us unless they adopt a comparative perspective and take into account the performance of other systems of higher education in other economically advanced countries. When considerations of this kind are borne in mind, there are a number of indicators of comparative performance which could be readily utilized to indicate relative success or failure of effort. Fielden and Lockwood's survey[50] of planning and management in British universities pointed out that much useful data was already available in most universities, but only one university in their sample was found to make a systematic presentation and analysis of simple things like staff-student ratios, student wastage, unit costs, space occupancy, percentage of research workers to U.G.C. financed staff, percentage distribution of income and expenditure, staff and student applications to places ratios, average number of library book issues per user, etc. The use of these and other indicators not only provide useful evidence of real trends and changes within a single institution over a time, but, if compared with others and with national figures, would make decision-making more informal and, hopefully, more realistic.

Our case is that criteria for measurement or evaluation should be more explicit. One should be aware of the limitations and crudity of some attempts at assessment. Nevertheless, present decisions are almost certainly taken on criteria which are cruder and more limited than those that would emerge from an explicit process of goal-formulation. Moreover, the process of goal-setting and evaluation by small groups is a method suited to crossing disciplinary and departmental boundaries. Activity and achievement through the workings of the problem-solving groups may be one of the few means remaining to bond together the seams of the modern 'pluralistic' university.

Suggestions for Further Reading

There are many books upon universities. Many are very specialized, however, and overall quality varies widely. The following is only a brief selection and is chosen partly for relevance to our theme and partly for appeal to the general reader.

For those who wish to know more about organizational analysis, an up-to-date introduction is David Bradley and Roy Wilkie: *The Concept of Organization,* Blackie, 1974, in this series. Other introductory works of value are C. Perrow: *Organizational Analysis,* Tavistock and Social Science Paperbacks, 1970; and A. Etzioni: *Modern Organizations,* Prentice Hall, 1964.

On universities, there is no book which adopts our organizational perspective. J. Fielden and G. Lockwood: *Planning and Management in Universities,* Chatto & Windus, 1973, will be a standard reference work on British universities for some time. A useful American work on a related theme is F. E. Rourke and G. E. Brooks: *The Managerial Revolution in Higher Education,* John Hopkins Press, 1966. More on an organizational note is N. J. Demerath, R. W. Stephens and R. R. Taylor: *Power, Presidents and Professors,* Basic Books, 1967, a section of which is a lively account of how the University of North Carolina at Chapel Hill changed from a 'patrimonial' to a 'bureaucratic' style of government. A more recent work, J. V. Baldridge: *Power and Conflict in the University,* Wiley, 1971, uses a 'political' model to analyse change at New York University.

As a general introduction, Clark Kerr: *The Uses of the*

118   *The University: An Organizational Analysis*

University, Harvard U.P., 1964, and Harper Torchbook, 1966, is still relevant. The collection of essays edited by David Martin: *Anarchy or Culture,* Routledge & Kegan Paul, 1969, is probably the best general view of the British scene.

Upon structures of government, all books are rather out of date. Sir James Mountford: *British Universities,* Oxford University Press, 1966, has merit, but the greatest assembly of factual data was the *Report of the Committee on Higher Education* ('Robbins' Committee) Cmnd. 2154, H.M.S.O., 1963, and its various appendices, particularly *Administrative, Financial and Economic Aspects of Higher Education,* Cmnd. 2154—IV, H.M.S.O., 1963.

On membership characteristics and academic staff, the standard work for many years will be A. H. Halsey and M. Trow: *The British Academics,* Faber, 1971. This work also contains a good general introduction. Another informative work is Harold Perkins: *Key Profession,* Routledge and Kegan Paul, 1969, a history of the Association of University Teachers.

On students, sociologists and all academics will learn from Joan Abbot: *Student Life in a Class Society,* Pergamon, 1971, but the general reader may find it too specialized. On student organization and disturbances, Sir Eric Ashby and Mary Anderson: *The Rise of the Student Estate in Britain,* Macmillan, 1970, and C. Crouch: *The Student Revolt,* the Bodley Head, 1970, are readable and informative. On American troubles, S. M. Lipset: *Rebellion in the University,* Routledge and Kegan Paul, 1972, is a worthwhile survey, and J. Searle: *The Campus War,* Penguin Books, 1972, is a well-written, if sometimes mistaken, polemic.

On administrators, apart from the 'university management' books noted above, J. Barzun: *The American University,* Oxford University Press, 1969, puts his case most eloquently.

On relations with the environment, R. O. Berdahl: *British Universities and the State,* Cambridge U.P., 1959, is the best historical background. The alleged danger to academic freedom from industry is spelled out in E. P. Thompson: *Warwick University Ltd.,* Penguin Books, 1970, and the threat to American universities from the research entrepreneurs and federal agencies is described in R. Nisbet: *The Degradation of the Academic Dogma,* Heinemann, 1971. The best single account however, of a university's relationships with its environment is W. H. Oliver's article on 'A society and its universities: the case of New Zealand' in J. Lawlor (ed): *The New University,* Routledge and Kegan Paul, 1968.

On the subject of 'problem-solving groups' mentioned in the last chapter, a useful introduction is R. R. Blake, H. A. Shepard, and J. S. Mouton: *Managing Intergroup Conflict in Industry,* Gulf, 1964. One case-study in a similar vein is A. J. Marrow, D. A. Bowers and S. E. Seashore: *Management by Participation,* Harper & Row, 1967. A comprehensive view is provided by a selection of articles in W. Bennis, K. D. Benne and R. Chin: *The Planning of Change,* 2nd edition, Holt, Rinehart & Winston, 1970.

References

1. John Henry, Cardinal Newman: *The Idea of a University,* Longman's, 1852; Preface 5th edition.
2. W. B. Gallie: *A New University: A. D. Lindsay and the Keele Experiment,* Chatto and Windus, 1960; p. 111.
3. A. Flexner: *Universities, American, English, German,* Oxford University Press, 1930; pp. 102–105.
4. Clark Kerr: *The Uses of the University,* Harper Torchbrook, 1966; p. 16.
5. Clark Kerr, as above; p. 20.
6. G. S. Jones: 'The Meaning of Student Revolt', in A. Cockburn and R. Blackburn (eds): *Student Power,* Penguin Books, 1969.
7. As 6.
8. Clark Kerr, as above; Chapter 1.
9. Clark Kerr, as above; p. 20.
10. J. V. Baldridge: *Power and Conflict in the University,* John Wiley & Son, 1971.
11. Cmnd. 2154: *Report of Committee on Higher Education,* H.M.S.O., 1963.
12. *The Guardian,* 1/11/72; p. 14, *Question of Degree,* extract from lecture.
13. *The Guardian,* 1/11/72, p. 14, *Question of Degree,* extract from lecture.
14. Cmnd. 2154: *Report,* pp. 6, 7.
15. A. Etzioni: *Modern Organizations,* Prentice-Hall, 1964; Chapter 2.
16. J. Barzun: *The American University,* Oxford University Press, 1969; p. 2.

17. Quoted in V. H. H. Green: *The Universities*, Penguin Books, 1969; p. 317.
18. *The Guardian*, 6/3/73, p. 21: *'Publish and be Raised'*, by S. Smith.
19. R. A. Nisbet: *The Degradation of the Academic Dogma*, Heinemann, 1971.
20. P. F. Drucker: *The Practice of Management*, Heinemann, 1955.
21. D. McGregor: *The Human Side of Enterprise*, McGraw-Hill, 1960.
22. John Humble: *Management by Objectives in Action*, McGraw-Hill, 1970.
23. D. C. Peltz and F. M. Andrews: *Scientists in Organizations*, Wiley, 1966; Chapter 2.
24. Cmnd. 2154: *Report*; p. 229.
25. Cmnd. 2154: *Report*; p. 229.
26. *Report of Review Body*, University of Birmingham, 1973.
27. A.U.T. *Bulletin*, No. 51, June 1973.
28. E. P. Thompson (ed): *Warwick University Ltd.*, Penguin, 1970; pp. 136–143.
29. Joan Woodward: *Industrial Organization: Theory and Practice*, Oxford University Press, 1965.
30. T. Burns and G. M. Stalker: *The Management of Innovation*, Tavistock, 1961.
31. A. K. Rice: *The Modern University*, Tavistock, 1970; pp. 81–87.
32. W. O. Hagstrom: *The Scientific Community*, Basic Books, 1965; p. 106.
33. D. C. Peltz and F. M. Andrews, as above.
34. See H. Baumgartel: 'Leadership Style as a Variable in Research Administration', *Administrative Science Quarterly*, Dec. 1967; pp. 344–60. Reprinted in C. Orth, et alia (eds): *Administering Research and Development*, Tavistock, 1965.
35. Sheldon Davis: 'An Organic Problem-Solving Method of Organizational Change' in *Journal of Applied Behavioural Science*, III, No. 1 (1967) reprinted in W. Bennis, et alia (eds): *The Planning of Change*, 2nd edition, Holt, Rinehart & Winston, 1970.
36. A. H. Halsey and M. Trow: *The British Academics*, Faber, 1971.

37. *The Observer*, 16/6/68; p. 21: *Crisis on the Campus*, by Ivan Yates.
38. Clark Kerr, as above.
39. R. A. Nisbet, as above.
40. Cmnd. 2154: *Report*; p. 221.
41. Clark Kerr, as above; pp. 29, 30.
42. J. Barzun, as above; p. 96.
43. Letter in *Times Higher Educational Supplement*, 8/6/73; p. 12.
44. *The Guardian*, 12/5/70; p. 11: *Sussex all at Sea*, by John Ezard.
45. C. Blake and S. McDowall: 'A Local Input-Output Table', *Scottish Journal of Political Economy*, Nov. 1967.
    M. Brownrigg: *A Study of Economic Input: The University of Stirling*, Scottish Academic Press, 1973.
46. F. M. M. Lewes and Anne Kirkness: *Exeter University and City*, Exeter University, 1973.
47. Cmnd. 2154; pp. 230–233.
48. Gareth Williams: 'University Recruitment 1968/9 and 1970/1', in *Universities Quarterly*, Spring 1973.
49. J. D. Mooney and A. C. Reilly: *Principles of Organization*, Harper, 1939.
50. J. Fielden and G. Lockwood: *Planning and Management in British Universities*, Chatto and Windus, 1973.

The Concept of Organization

Roy Wilkie and David Bradley

Organizations rule our lives. *The Concept of Organization* asks some important questions about the workings of these structures and takes a critical look at the roles they play in our society. This book provides a lucid introduction to the field of organizational studies, explores the composition, attributes and goals of organizations, and investigates the behaviour of human beings within these environments.

Without resorting to obscure technical language, the authors clarify current trends and attitudes in the increasingly important field of organization theory. They supply models of this theory at work by examining the organizational problems of Arts Council-subsidized theatres in Britain.

The Concept of Organization will prove to be a valuable tool for social science students, for businessmen and working administrators, and for everyone concerned with the dominance of large scale organizations in our society.

David Bradley was educated at Woolwich Polytechnic. Since October 1966 he has been lecturing in the Department of Administration, University of Strathclyde.

Roy Wilkie was educated at the University of Aberdeen. Since October 1967 he has been Reader in the Department of Administration, University of Strathclyde.

The Hospital:
An Organizational Analysis

Stephen Green

Hospitals have played a part at some time or another in everyone's life. Yet we know little about what goes on behind their sterile masks and concealing screens. This book looks at the hospital from the viewpoint of organization theory. It examines the influence which the medical, political and social environment has upon its functioning and considers the ways in which the goal of patient care may be subverted. Stephen Green takes a critical look at the power of the medical profession, and the power bases held by the different occupational groups in the hospital. He investigates the problems of control and co-ordination within the structure of the institution.

How does the hospital cope with the presence of independent professionals? What problems do the uncertainties of patient care and medical technology create? How does the hospital deal with their difficulties? This introductory analysis of the hospital as an organization illuminates many of the crucial issues that beset our health care system today.